ON MISSION WITH GOD

Living God's Purpose *for* His Glory

ON MISSION WITH GOD

Living God's Purpose *for* His Glory

HENRY T. BLACKABY
AVERY T. WILLIS, JR.

BROADMAN
&HOLMAN
PUBLISHERS

Nashville, Tennessee

0-8054-2553-5
Published by Broadman & Holman Publishers, Nashville, Tennessee
The authors are represented by the literary agency of Wolgemuth & Associates, Inc.

Dewey Decimal Classification: 266
Subject Heading: CHRISTIAN LIVING

Library of Congress Cataloging-in-Publication Data

Blackaby, Henry T., 1935–
    On mission with God : living God's purpose for His glory / Henry Blackaby and
    Avery T. Willis, Jr.
    p. cm.
    ISBN 0-8054-2553-5
    1. Missions. 2. God—Will. 3. Providence and government of God. I. Willis,
    Avery T. II. Title.
    BV2061.3 .B57 2002
    266—dc21
                                                                    2001043644

1 2 3 4 5 6 7 8 9 10 06 05 04 03 02

CONTENTS

PUBLISHER'S FOREWORD

GOD IS MOVING IN UNPRECEDENTED AND EXCITING WAYS THROUGHOUT the world today. And He is calling all Christians to join Him on His mission.

On Mission with God is a book about God and His mission. Mission is God's activity; missions describes the activity of God's people.

God isn't interested in just giving Christians a missions experience. He is interested in Christians' being on mission with Him. The distinction is more than subtle. It is earth-shattering! Fully comprehended, this concept has the potential to radically alter and revitalize the church today. The reason this book is so revolutionary is that it calls for altering the way Christians view God's perspective on the whole world today and the participation of all Christians in reaching the world.

God reveals Himself to us so we can adjust our lives to His. He wants to reveal His glory to a waiting world through us. He does that only when we completely allow Him to manifest Himself through us. As we experience God on mission, we do not choose our assignments. He does. Our ultimate goal is to allow God to reveal Himself through us as He did through the people of the Bible.

God's mission knows no geographic boundaries, nor is it bound by a calendar. God lives and works in eternity, but He also works within time. He has been at work in our world since the dawn of creation. He is at work today. He will be at work until the day comes when representatives from every tribe, tongue, nation, and people on the face of the earth are gathered around His throne worshiping Him.

Neither Henry Blackaby nor Avery Willis remembers their first meeting although they have been the closest of friends for many years. Their first significant personal interaction came at a National Lay Renewal Conference. After both spoke on discovering where God was at work and joining Him, Avery told Henry, "I believe God has given you a message greatly needed by the church. I will do all I can to help you get it published."

The rest is history, as *Experiencing God: Knowing and Doing the Will of God* rocked the Christian world. A few years later God gave Henry the message of *Fresh Encounter: God's Pattern for Revival and Spiritual Awakening*. It was first a video presentation and a book of Henry and Avery sharing the message. Henry added the prominent theme of "God on Mission" and told the story of how Israel had refused to be on mission with God. Then he laid out the steps of how God's people stray from God and how they can come back to God and join Him on mission to bring spiritual awakening and world redemption.

Millions of people have had their lives radically changed while studying the books *Experiencing God* and *Fresh Encounter*. So why write another book dealing with the same theme? First, because so many have experienced God in fresh ways they are ready for a next step. Second, because the mission of

Experiencing God was not spelled out in the original book—there was nothing at the end of the arrow of Henry's chalkboard diagram.

Avery proposed that they work together on a book that spells out the mission of God and explains the goal that God has for His people in the world. In the seven intervening years, Avery has served as senior vice president for Overseas Operations of the International Mission Board of the Southern Baptist Convention. Henry began to broaden the scope of his ministry by serving as special assistant to the presidents of LifeWay Christian Resources, the North American Mission Board, and the International Mission Board. Then he branched out in many other ways through the Henry Blackaby Ministries. Henry and Avery began to explore the message in scores of opportunities as they continued to work together. On an Alaskan cruise, they shared the message of the Seven Spiritual Markers that is a prominent section of each chapter of this book with several hundred participants. Then they shared the complete message in this book at the International Missions Week at LifeWay's Conference Center at Glorieta, and literally around the world in conferences where they spoke.

However, because of their ministering continually around the world together with their other duties, they were not able to write the book. By this time they had tapes of scores of sermons, Bible studies, conversations, transcripts, and first drafts that Avery had written, but neither could carve out enough time to finish the book. Three people helped write the interactive book *On Mission with God: Living God's Purpose for His Glory*. Lisa Sells helped write the first version of chapters 1 and 2 and helped broaden the scope of each character. Muriel Evans took all the material and drafted a first version. Henry added his input. Avery reworked the material. Louis Moore condensed and edited this volume of material into an interactive book with manageable daily studies for each week. For this version of that book Avery and Henry added new material, and Louis then drafted it.

So what should you expect God to do in your life as you read this book? You will see the Bible from an overall perspective that you may never have seen before. You will see your individual experience from God's perspective of your entire life and as a part of His corporate people. You will see the world from God's global perspective. You will experience the heart of God as you join in glorifying Him among all peoples.

Henry and Avery say, "Our prayer is that God will do the same work in your heart that He did in ours as we studied God's mission from many perspectives as we traveled to all the continents except Antarctica. We offer what He has taught us for your consideration. If you are helped by it, then give the glory to God. Although many have helped us communicate the message, we know that God gave it to us. We hope we have communicated it clearly and accept full accountability for the content.

"We cannot thank each of the persons involved in this effort enough for all the work they have done to make this contribution to the body of Christ. As you read you will notice that the book is written from a first person perspective to prevent the awkwardness of switching back and forth between two persons. But Henry and Avery jointly take full responsibility for the ideas and concepts they present in this book."

All royalties from this book will go into a trust fund with the income from it being used to translate, publish, and distribute books by the authors in other languages for the peoples of the world.

—Broadman & Holman Publishers

1

A ROAD MAP FOR THE JOURNEY

For from Him and through Him and to Him are
all things. To Him be the glory forever, amen.
—Romans 11:36

THE TROPICAL SUN BEAT DOWN ON MY VAN AS MY WIFE AND
I wound through the dusty roads of East Java, Indonesia. For an
hour I had looked for a village on the unmarked road. Finally I
stopped and asked a man where the village was.

He replied, "Kesana," which, loosely translated, means "that-
away." He pointed down the road with his thumb in the polite
Javanese manner. I followed up with questions about how far it
was, how I would know where to turn, and how I would know
when I got to my destination.

After reiterating, "Kesana," several times, he said, "I'll show
you," and hopped in the car. I protested that he would be
stranded several miles from where he was going. He insisted that
he could get back. Now it was easy. All I had to do was to turn

when he told me and stop when we arrived. I had asked for a road map, but instead, I got a personal guide!

When you ask God for a road map for your life, He replies, "I am the way. I will personally lead you. Follow Me, obey My commands, and I will get you to the destination." On the way you discover that you may not get to the destination you first had in mind, but you will get to His destination for your life—a much better arrival point than you had planned.

That's what it means to be on mission with God. You let Him be your guide and direct you because you believe that He has a purpose for your life. That purpose is not just for your own personal benefit but for His purpose and His mission.

As you look at the diagram on page 19, you see that you experience God as you obey Him and join Him on mission. This diagram answers the question, What is the mission of God? God's mission is that the "earth will be filled with the knowledge of the glory of the LORD, as the waters cover the sea" (Hab. 2:14). As you read this book, think of God's mission as what He does—His purpose. Think of God's glory as who He is—His presence. Put them together in your personal experience, and you will be *living God's purpose for His glory.*

God does not merely sit on a throne in heaven. He is always at His work everywhere to fulfill His purpose. Jesus said, "My Father is still working, and I also am working" (John 5:17). This book is about God's mission. God is moving to accomplish His mission that all peoples will know His glory (Hab. 2:14, Phil. 2:10–11, Eph. 1:9–12, 1 Cor. 15:24–28). As you join Him on mission, you experience God and the glory of His presence.

2

Make no mistake, there is a difference between *mission* and *missions*. By *mission*, I mean the total redemptive purpose of God to establish His kingdom. *Missions*, on the other hand, is the activity of God's people—the church—to proclaim and to demonstrate the kingdom of God cross-culturally to the world.

This book focuses on God's mission rather than on our missions. God isn't interested in merely giving you a missions experience but in your being on mission with Him. This book does not attempt to call you to be a missionary. Our desire is to help you understand the heart of God and His mission.

God reveals Himself to you so you can adjust your life to Him and join Him on His mission. Where He takes you is His doing, not ours. He wants to reveal His glory to a waiting world through you. He can do that anywhere He chooses when you allow Him to manifest Himself through you. As you experience God on mission, you do not choose your experiences, your assignment, or your location. He does. Your ultimate goal is to allow God to reveal Himself to you and then through you to others.

When I was looking for the East Java village where I planned to share the gospel, I was on mission with God. My family and I were the only missionaries living among eight to nine million people. I thought I would be on mission there for years, but God had other plans. Within months He directed us to Central Java to teach in a seminary, where I eventually became president as part of God's purpose for me in His mission.

Being on mission is not a profession, a vocation, or a location. I was nineteen when I committed my life to be on mission with God. I have since worked in a variety of professions—laborer in a milling company, salesperson, volunteer director of a rescue

3

mission, pastor, missionary, professor, author, director of adult discipleship for my denomination, and currently, overseas vice president of my denomination's International Mission Board leading our more-than five thousand missionaries. When was I most on mission with God? Actually, in every case. No doubt, I followed closer and obeyed God more at some times than others, but still I was on mission with God all the time.

Henry Blackaby, my coauthor, had a similar experience, as you will learn later. However, Henry and his wife, Marilynn, committed themselves to be missionaries, only to be turned down because of their son's health. They ended up back in Canada, Henry's birthplace. Henry was pastor of a small church there. During that time Marilynn experienced difficulty in understanding what being on mission with God meant. Marilynn recalls, "Henry traveled a lot; I was at home with our four boys. I remember asking myself after a long day of washing dishes, cooking meals, and running after kids: Is this being a missionary? Later, as I was vacuuming, God answered my question: 'Yes, Marilynn, it is. This is your mission field.' And with that realization my daily work took on a different meaning because I knew without a doubt that it was what God had given me to do.'"[1]

Our hope is that this book will bring you face-to-face with God and what it means to glorify Him by being on mission with Him before a watching world.

THE SEVEN

The Bible is a book about God. Why then is 60 percent of its stories about people? Because God has chosen to reveal Himself through people. The Bible includes stories of people who interacted with God and His mission, either for good or bad. God included only the stories that reveal Himself and His ways as He interacted with them. God reveals Himself in the Bible as He interacts with people so that you can know Him and join Him on mission.

God also knows that we learn best through stories of real people who experience real problems in a tough world. The Bible pulls no punches—it tells about the warts, sins, and failures of its heroes along with their victories.

You experience God as you meet Him and interact with Him in real life. You do not have to base your experiences on capricious circumstances or emotional highs. Base them on the eternal truths of God revealed in the Bible. God reveals Himself, His purpose, and His ways through the lives of the people He has included in the Holy Book. You can depend on God's revelation to you through the Bible.

Let me ask you another question: Since God reveals Himself and His truth through people in the Bible, if you understood what God revealed through the seven most significant characters of the Bible, would you have a standard for understanding God's mission? We believe you would.

When God is about to do something, He takes the initiative and comes to one or more of His servants. He lets them know what He is about to do. He invites them to adjust their lives to Him, so He can accomplish His mission through them. Since we can't examine the lives of everyone in the Bible, we will look in depth at the lives of the seven most significant people in the Bible—Abraham, Moses, David, Jesus, Peter, Paul, and John—to see how God used their lives to shape His redemptive mission to all peoples. You might want to include others as we do, but we choose these when limited to seven. Each moved and reflected God's kingdom purpose in his day. They joined God on mission, and through them the Holy Spirit helps us understand what God is doing today.

When I think of a bird's-eye view of the whole Bible and its most significant persons, I think of a trip my wife and I took to Nepal to visit missionaries who were experiencing a tremendous response to the gospel. I had always wanted to see the Himalayan mountain range at the "top of the world" that extends in a massive arc for about fifteen hundred miles and includes more than thirty peaks rising to heights greater than twenty-four thousand feet. We took a small plane and saw a panorama of eight of the world's ten highest peaks, including Mount Everest, the world's highest peak at 29,023 feet! Mount Everest is awesome! When I compare this mountain range to the main characters of the Bible, I see Jesus as the highest peak. But ascending toward Him from either side are other peaks that point to His grandeur—men and women of the Bible through whom God revealed Himself and His mission. In addition to studying Jesus' life, we will examine three persons from the Old Testament and three from the New Testament, each of whom points to Christ.

Each year *Time* magazine designates a Man or Woman of the Year. In the year 2000 *Time* gave a Person of the Century award. That person was Albert Einstein. But *Time* also gave a Person of the Century award to one person in each of the preceding nine centuries: Thomas Edison, nineteenth century; Thomas Jefferson, eighteenth; Sir Isaac Newton, seventeenth; Queen Elizabeth I, sixteenth; Johannes Gutenberg, fifteenth; Giotto, the Italian painter, fourteenth; Genghis Khan, thirteenth; the warrior Saladin, twelfth; and William the Conqueror, eleventh.

Time said these were the greatest nine men and one woman of the last thousand years—the most famous people of the last millennium. Many other people have lived and died in the last thousand years, but I would put the seven characters in this book ahead of any of them. Through them God revealed His eternal mission. Just think how many lives these persons have influenced! After this I will refer to them as the Seven—your mentors on mission with God.

If you have other characters you would like to learn about, you may use the pattern we will show you to study how God works with people. Our thesis is this: If you know what God has revealed through these seven biblical characters, you will understand God's heart and mission. Look what God revealed through the Seven:

- Through *Abraham* God revealed Himself as the Lord, the Almighty Provider who wants to bless all the peoples of the world through His people.
- Through *Moses* God revealed Himself as the I AM THAT I AM whose plan is to show His glory to the world through His people who are to be a kingdom of priests to all peoples.
- Through *David* God revealed that his seed would rule all nations and His kingdom would be for all peoples.
- Through *Jesus* God revealed His love and His purpose to reconcile the world to Himself and to send His disciples as ministers of reconciliation to all peoples.

7

- Through *Peter* God demonstrated how the Holy Spirit would empower His people to be His witnesses to all peoples.
- Through *Paul* God revealed the mystery of the ages that He includes all peoples in His redemption and sends missionaries to all nations, tribes, tongues, and peoples.
- Through *John* God revealed that all nations, tribes, tongues, and peoples will worship and glorify Him forever in heaven.

As you look at God's mission through the eyes of His servants, be assured that it is God who is on mission. It is His mission, not ours. But He has determined to accomplish His mission through His people. He is actively working to involve His people with all the peoples of the world so they may know Him and worship Him. God's mission will be accomplished when Christ delivers the kingdom to the Father. Meanwhile, He gives us the opportunity to be on mission with Him so He can exalt the Son and draw all peoples to worship Him.

FOUR PERSPECTIVES

We will look at each of our seven mentors from four different perspectives. In each case you will be able to evaluate your own life from each of these same perspectives:

- *The Close-up Perspective.* In the first perspective we will examine each character's initial personal experiences with God using the Seven Realities of Experiencing God represented by the top of one peak in a mountain range.

- *The Wide-Angle Perspective.* Next we will back up so you can view the entire mountain which represents the character's lifetime of experiences with God and note the Seven Spiritual Markers that God uses with His people.
- *The 180-Degree Extra Wide-Angle Perspective.* Come on up higher and get an extra wide-angle view of how this character will influence the people of God to be on mission with God.
- *The 360-Degree Eternal Perspective.* The fourth perspective gives us an eternal view of how God sees His mission being revealed through this character from eternity.

Now let us introduce to you what we mean by each of these perspectives so you can anticipate how they will be experienced by the Seven and by you as God carries out His mission through each of us.

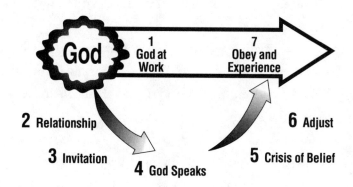

THE CLOSE-UP PERSPECTIVE OF EXPERIENCING GOD PERSONALLY

All through the Bible God reveals Himself to you so you can know Him personally. If you've studied *Experiencing God: Knowing and Doing the Will of God,* you already know the Seven Realities in the diagram on page 9.

You may have wondered if the Seven Realities in *Experiencing God* are eternal truths that apply to all people—or apply just to Moses. In this book you will see how God uses these same Seven Realities to reveal His glory in the lives of the Seven. And you will see how these Seven Realities also apply to your own life.

As we begin our journey on mission with God, let's review the Seven Realities taught in *Experiencing God.* God is at work all the time, and He initiates a personal, loving relationship with you and invites you to join Him in His work. As God speaks to you, you experience a crisis of belief that calls for major adjustments in your life so you can relate to Him and His mission. As you make the adjustments and obey Him, He moves you into the middle of His activity. You then are a part of God's mission.

God took the initiative with the Seven featured in this book. They did not come to God saying, "What great thing can I do for you?" Instead, God came to them and told them what He was about to do and invited them to be a part of it.

God encountered each one and told him what his role would be. God promised Abraham that he would begin a race of people who would bless all peoples. This same pattern is true for the other characters. God told Moses that he was to deliver His people from slavery and guide them to the promised land. God introduced David to the idea of a kingdom that would have no end. God told Peter that He would empower His people to witness to all peoples. Likewise God led Paul to break out of Judaism and take the gospel to all peoples. God showed John that He wants representatives of all peoples someday to worship Him. In each case God's activity was not the person's agenda. God revealed what He was doing and invited the person to join Him.

You may have thought you were saved just to go to heaven when you die, but God says, "I saved you to be on mission with Me to redeem a broken world. I'm bringing you back to My original mission, where you will participate in My purpose of redeeming and reconciling a lost world to Me." As you follow Christ, the Master sets the direction and tells you where He is and where He is going. Where the Master is, the servant must be. The servant responds—not initiates.

As we were taping the videos that accompany the interactive edition of this book, Henry spontaneously said: "When I was a nine-year-old boy, I had an encounter with God that was unique to a nine-year-old in which He convinced me beyond a question that He was God and I was not. That encounter changed the rest of my life. I never enter into His presence without that awareness. He is God and I am not. So He has access to my life. I don't tell Him what I want to do for Him. When God places me somewhere, it never crosses my mind to question. Or when a circumstance comes to my life, I recognize that He is God and I am not. I don't demand why. I just say, 'If you want to tell me, you will. You are God, and I am not.' After that encounter, everything in my life was changed, and I have never gotten over it."

Heeding God's invitation and responding positively will require major adjustments on your part. When God is about to redeem the world, what should you be doing? Can you imagine what the Seven would say if you could eavesdrop on them at the Starburst Coffee Shop on the corner of Praise Avenue and Hallelujah Boulevard up in heaven talking about the major adjustments they were asked to make back on earth? It might go something like this:

Abraham: My family and I were happy living in Ur of the Chaldees. I didn't ask God to send me to another country. He encountered me and told me this was what I was to do to reveal His glory to all the peoples of the earth. Can you imagine how I had to explain that to Sarah?

Moses: I was content to be living in the desert far away from my troubles in Egypt. I didn't go looking for that burning bush and the glory of God's presence. I certainly did not want to go back to Egypt for any sort of showdown with Pharaoh. God had to do a job on me to get me to join Him.

David: I was the baby in my family. Nobody ever took me that seriously until Samuel came to our home one day. I would have loved to spend my days tending sheep, playing my harp, and writing songs. I could never have imagined what God was going to do in and through my life.

Jesus: I had to leave my throne in heaven and empty Myself when My Father said I needed to give Myself to demonstrate His glory and to redeem all peoples. It would have been easier to stay there permanently. But I knew that the cross was ordained for Me before the foundation of the world.

Peter: I had a lot of trouble learning to be on mission with God. How could God use a brash fisherman like me to impact the world? Even self-confidence got in my way. I later learned that it was only with God's strength that I could really do anything. But when I finally caught on, God was able to do far more through me than I could have imagined.

Paul: I thought I was on mission with God on the road to Damascus trying to stamp out the spreading Christian wildfire when You, Jesus, encountered me and showed me Your glory. You turned me around, and the rest of my life was a whale of an adventure as I discovered what it really means to be on mission with God.

John: My mother wanted the best for me and for my brother James. And she taught us to strive for the best, also. What Jesus taught me was—he who is the greatest among you must be the servant of all. I would never have written the script for my life that He wrote, but I realize now He really did know best.

When God encounters you, He wants one thing—for you to join Him on His mission. God is not some genie in a bottle to grant your every wish and desire. He doesn't enter your life to pamper you or indulge you. He comes to involve you in the greatest adventure of life—experiencing His glory as you accompany Him on His mission. By joining Him on His mission, you will experience God and be forever changed in the process. You are not just a channel through which God does something, but you are a transformed part of His eternal purpose to make you and all peoples of the world like His Son for His glory.

Now let's review how God reveals Himself and His glory from the three other perspectives.

THE WIDE-ANGLE PERSPECTIVE OF YOUR WHOLE LIFE

After you have examined a character from the close-up initial experience with God, then we need to step back and see how the Seven and your life look to God from a lifetime perspective. With this Wide-Angle Perspective we'll use the mountain-range analogy to see the whole mountain of your life, not just a single experience. Most of the time we are so involved in what is happening at the peak of our experiences with God that we have only fleeting thoughts about the impact of our whole lives on others. I have noticed that when people talk about persons who have impacted their lives, they talk more about the life message of the person even though they illustrate it with specific experiences.

Being on mission with God means experiencing God all your life! When you someday step back and look at your life as you complete it on earth, you will find it fascinating to see what God was doing with you throughout your lifetime. The Lord wants to show you more of His purpose—not just for today but for all of your life.

Looking at the Spiritual Markers in your life can help you see the direction God is pointing your life. A Spiritual Marker is a time when you knew that you experienced God and did His will. When I asked T. W. Hunt, a spiritual giant, to move to LifeWay Christian Resources and lead in prayer ministries, he had a difficult time leaving the seminary where he had taught for twenty-four years. I knew he was about to visit Vancouver, B.C., where Henry Blackaby was serving. "Henry has helped a lot of people know God's will," I told him. "Why don't you talk to him?" He did. Henry told him to look at his Spiritual Markers—times when he was sure that God had spoken. Then see if these Spiritual Markers lined up to point to a decision in this matter. Even though it was a radical vocational change for T. W., the Spiritual Markers did line up, and for many years he served powerfully in that role at LifeWay as a prayer leader for his denomination and many others.

I want to introduce to you Seven Spiritual Markers that all people experience if they follow thorough on God's initiatives. The diagram below pictures these. The Seven Realities that you studied earlier in this chapter may be repeated over and over during each of these Seven Spiritual Markers as you have a continuing relationship with God.

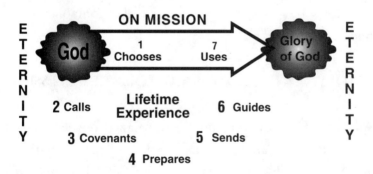

Spiritual Marker #1: God chooses you to involve you in His mission to reconcile the world to Himself. When you read the Scriptures about God choosing the Seven, would you say God's choices were accidental, coincidental, or providential? Every time you see God's choice in the Bible, you become aware that it is providential and relates to what He wants to do through that person.

Spiritual Marker #2: God calls you to Himself so you can be on mission with Him. What do we mean when we say a person is called? To many modern Christians, *called* means that one is to enter a Christian vocation. To God, *called* means your life in Christ is your vocation no matter what you do to earn a living (Luke 9:23; Eph. 4:1). At salvation God calls you to a relationship with Him; He also calls you to service; and He calls you to fulfill His mission for your life.

Spiritual Marker #3: God initiates a covenant of promise and obedience with you in order to accomplish His mission. God makes covenants with those He calls. God initiates a covenant of promise, obedience, and blessing with you. In this book you'll discover that God made covenants with all of the Seven. He made promises to them dependent on their obedience. Look at the equation below. If you leave out one of the components, what happens?

$$COVENANT \neq PROMISE + OBEDIENCE = BLESSING!$$

All parts of the equation must be in balance for the covenant to work. God writes all covenants. They are not negotiating sessions. You can't bargain with Him and fulfill His mission. He wrote the covenant and asks you to agree to it. God's covenants are permanent—for His glory and your good and the good of all peoples.

Spiritual Marker #4: God prepares and equips you to be on mission with Him. God prepares you to fulfill His mission in your life. Part of your preparation is a fundamental desire to shape your character to match your assignment. God took many years to shape the character of each of the Seven. The bigger the assignment, the longer or more challenging the circumstances He used to prepare them.

God spent forty years readying Abraham to be the father of faith, who believed God enough to offer his son. God took eighty years to prepare Moses to lead the Israelites out of slavery. David spent ten of the worst years of his life after he was anointed to be king because God needed to prepare him to establish His kingdom instead of his own. Peter spent every day for three years with Jesus in preparation, but God had to keep preparing him for another ten years before he was able and willing to lead the church to be on mission to the Gentiles. God sent Paul to Arabia for three years of personal training, ten years in his hometown of Tarsus and another year in Antioch with Barnabas before He sent him on his first missionary trip. God waited until John was age ninety before He used him to write the Gospel of John and the Revelation.

Take note of what God is doing in your life right now because He is preparing you for your assignment. Your next assignment may occur tomorrow, and your ultimate assignment may be twenty years from now, but God is preparing you according to His foreknowledge and wisdom. When He puts you in a situation that calls for preparation, you can be sure He has already equipped you to handle it by His grace. The adversity you face today is preparation for your assignment tomorrow.

Spiritual Marker #5: God sends you where He can best work through you to accomplish His mission. Each of the Seven reflected God's kingdom purpose and influenced his generation by moving to the place where God had planned to bless and use him. They really did see where God was at work.

God sent Abraham to a far country, Moses back to his own people, David from the country to the city, Jesus from heaven to earth, Peter to all peoples in his own country, Paul to the Gentiles out on the edge, and John to a faraway island. Each of the Seven had a different destination as he joined God on mission. One of them could not do the work of any of the others. God knows where to send you to accomplish His mission through you.

God is establishing His kingdom locally, globally, and eternally. Only God can determine where you go—unless you think you are smarter than God is or you have your best interests at heart more than He does! Jonah thought he knew his assignment better than God did; look what happened to him!

Spiritual Marker #6: God guides you step by step on His mission to glorify Him among all peoples. God's guidance is critical to your joining Him on mission. The place is not the only important thing. The way He gets you to that place is also important. For example, during Paul's two years in jail in Caesarea, He got to witness to King Agrippa and Felix. Then he appeared before Caesar in Rome. While in prison Paul had time to write letters to the churches; those letters now make up almost half of the New Testament. This was all in God's plan. When the going gets tough, just be sure that God is guiding you each step of the way.

Spiritual Marker #7: God uses you to fulfill His mission in your lifetime for His glory. How does God want to use you to bring glory to Him during your lifetime? Imagine how you will view your life the day after you die. History records the lives of people who have made a difference. But because time and worldly values bind historians, they cannot see all God is accomplishing through the heroes of faith. Many of the heroes in the Hall of Faith in Hebrews 11 would not make *Time* magazine's Heroes of the Millennium, but you can be sure they are recorded in the pages of heaven's books. Your influence will not stop when you die. Only eternity will reveal your significance.

THE 180-DEGREE PERSPECTIVE OF INFLUENCE ON THE PEOPLE OF GOD IN YOUR GENERATION

God was doing something greater than just working in the lives of the Seven. His plan was to influence an entire people! Through the lives of each individual, God was shaping a people in his generation to do His will and carry out His mission.

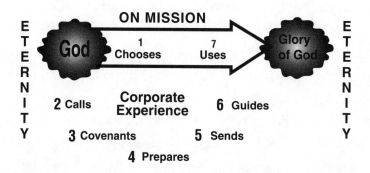

God designed us to function together as a chosen generation, a holy nation, and a royal kingdom of priests so that we "may proclaim the praises of the One who called you out of darkness into His marvelous light" (1 Pet. 2:9; Exod. 19:4–6). When God invites you to join Him on mission, He invites you to function as a member of that body. As God reconciles us to Himself, He reconciles us to one another—churches, races, and a broken world. The stronger and more complete the interdependence in the body, the sooner His mission will be done.

The Great Commission is Christ's corporate covenant with all His disciples. If He gave the commission to the disciples as individuals, then it died when they did. If He gave it to them as the church, it lasts until accomplished. God brought your church into being to join Him on His mission to take the gospel to the ends of the earth.

THE 360-DEGREE PERSPECTIVE FROM ETERNITY

In this last perspective we will put God's mission into the context of eternity. God moves from eternity to eternity. (See the diagram on page 15.) God lives in eternity but created time when He created the earth and its twenty-four-hour orbit around the sun. Time is a capsule for our sake—not His. Time takes its significance from eternity. He reveals Himself to us in time, and He works in time to carry out His eternal mission. We tend to think the whole meaning of life is about us, our time, and how little time we have, but God works for His eternal purpose. God is involving His people in His mission so everyone will glorify Him in everything. He wants His name celebrated in all generations.

If you studied the book *Experiencing God*, you realized that there was nothing at the end of the arrow in the diagram. You were left to interpret where the arrow pointed. One of the primary reasons for this book is to demonstrate that the mission of God is for all peoples to glorify God.

The story of the Bible is the story of God's glory! The mission of God is that all peoples glorify Him. Glorifying God is God-centered, not people-centered. All the wonderful things you experience—your redemption, your salvation, and your understanding of His love—are for the purpose of glorifying Him.

God is the most God-centered being in the universe (Isa. 45:21–25). He is jealous of His holy name (Josh. 24:19–20). He saved the Israelites for His own sake (Isa. 48:9–12). He saves us for His glory (Jude 24–25). He says that the reason all people will confess Jesus as Lord is the glory of the Father (Phil. 2:10–11).

If you have difficulty with God's wanting everyone and everything to glorify Him, that's your problem, not God's. Look at it this way. All of us have One whom we can glorify and worship. God can't look up to anyone else or worship anything, or He would be breaking the first commandment! He can't worship lesser gods, because they are not gods! He doesn't have an equal. Who else could He, in all good conscience, recommend for you to worship, other than Himself? God is complete in Himself. God knows you will find your greatest joy and fulfillment in worshiping Him.

God is on mission to do three things so that all peoples will glorify Him.

First, God is reconciling the world to Himself through Jesus Christ. God is gearing all things toward gathering in the harvest. In these last days the Spirit of God is stirring the church to respond to God's great purpose so that all peoples will glorify Him throughout eternity. More people and more churches are praying and adopting unreached people groups. They are no longer content merely to give money. They want to be involved in completing what Christ said in Matthew 24:14, "This good news of the kingdom will be proclaimed in all the world as a testimony to all nations. And then the end will come." They believe this is the time to "make known his deeds among the nations," so all peoples will join in praising and exalting God.

Second, God is bringing all things together under one head—Jesus Christ. Ephesians 1:9–10 says, "He made known to us the mystery of his will, according to his good pleasure, which he purposed in Christ, to be put into effect when the times will have reached their fulfillment—to bring all things in heaven and on earth together under one head, even Christ" (NIV). The words *bring together* in Greek mean to "sum up," like adding a column of figures, except the Greeks put the sum at the top of the list instead of at the bottom. God made Christ the head; everything in heaven and earth will be put under Him.

God's mission will be accomplished through the church so those in the heavenly realm will know how great God's wisdom is. God will drop us as His people into the middle of His mission, and we will experience God's full presence and power as He reconciles all things to Himself. But more important than that, Ephesians 3:10 says, "His intent was that now, through the church, the manifold wisdom of God should be made known to the rulers and authorities in the heavenly realms" (NIV). That is incredible! Satan and his evil cohorts think God is foolish to work with fallen humans to show His glory. But God is turning the tables, and the church will finally be His exhibit B to show His wisdom.

Did that last statement surprise you? If the church is God's exhibit B, what is exhibit A? It is Christ who "disarmed the rulers and authorities and disgraced them publicly; He triumphed over them by Him" (Col. 2:15). God's eternal purpose is accomplished in Christ through His church to the world for His glory. He places everything under the feet of His Son. Joining God on mission is simply being involved with God as He reconciles all things to Himself through Christ. God put everything under Christ's feet in order to reconcile everything to Himself (Eph. 1:21–22).

Third, God is bringing all peoples to worship Him. The Book of Revelation is replete with glory and praise to the One who is "all in all." The great Alpha and Omega will rule and reign eternally over the new heaven and the new earth. We will join the angelic hosts and the unnumbered peoples around the throne giving God praise for all eternity. That is your motive to be on mission with God while you are here in time—that in the eternal beyond you might experience men and women from every nation on the face of the earth praising God around His throne. Nothing less and nothing else will satisfy the great heart of God and bring Him the glory that He deserves through eternity!

Look what God is doing now to get us where we will be then. At no time in history have so many diverse peoples and nations intersected in so many ways. Globalization has made it possible that with a push of the remote control or a click of a mouse, you can know anything about any place on the globe. Travel and mobility have put more ethnic diversity in your backyard than your grandparents ever thought imaginable. This interaction is as significant as any decision God has orchestrated in your personal life.

Have you ever asked why at this particular point in human history God is allowing people from all over the world to intermingle and mix in unprecedented ways? The Internet has coined a new word that is a combination of globalization and localization—"glocalization." The church must be global and local at the same time! (Acts 1:8). I believe God is intertwining us locally and globally so we Christians can be His witnesses to all peoples. He has placed you in this unique era of His kingdom's advance because He wants you to join Him on mission to bring all peoples of the world to glorify His name. In this book you are learning how and why. You will learn new insights as you walk through the corridors of history with seven men who had feet of clay but kept their eyes on eternity.

God has purposed to see His name proclaimed among the nations. He is providing you the opportunity to join Him in seeing His glory fill heaven and earth.

2

ABRAHAM ON MISSION WITH GOD

A BLESSING FOR ALL PEOPLES

"I will make you into a great nation and I will
bless you; I will make your name great, and you will
be a blessing. I will bless those who bless you, and
whoever curses you I will curse; and all peoples on
earth will be blessed through you."
—Genesis 12:2–3

CAN YOU RECALL A TIME IN YOUR LIFE WHEN YOU INSTINCTIVELY
knew that you were making a decision that would affect your
entire life? I experienced such an occurrence when I was on state-
side assignment after I served for fourteen years as a missionary
in Indonesia.

Soon after I arrived in the United States, I began to experience
God encountering me in different ways than I had previously.

Besides being asked to present the typical missions emphases that missionaries make, I was also being asked at every turn to help train my denomination's churches and agencies in witnessing, discipleship, leadership training, and renewal. Three denominational agencies asked if I could remain in the United States permanently and work with them. All these requests confused me because I had planned to be a missionary for the rest of my life. I was happy in serving as president of the Indonesian Baptist Theological Seminary and in being used by God in many other ways.

Month after month I wrote in my journal, "Lord, I don't know what You are saying, but I sense that You are telling me that You want to do something else in my life." I also said, "Lord, I can't believe You would call a missionary back from Indonesia to serve in the United States when the total number of evangelical missionaries in Indonesia is 325 for 150 million people. God, find someone here who can disciple believers to serve You."

As God stirred me, He also showed me promises of what He would do if I obeyed Him. My wife, Shirley, and I set aside a day for fasting and prayer. He clearly showed us in Isaiah 43:18, "Forget the former things; do not dwell on the past."

That verse was like an arrow through my heart. I knew God was telling me I wouldn't return to Indonesia. Through my tears I said, "God, I can't bear not going back to Indonesia. So if that is what You are saying, You will have to bear it." Then after gaining my composure, I read on, "See, I am doing a new thing! Now it springs up; do you not perceive it? . . . I provide water in the desert and streams in the wasteland, to give drink to my people, my chosen, the people I formed for myself that they may proclaim my praise" (Isa. 43:19–21). I saw that God wanted to form (disciple) His people to proclaim His praise.

Then God showed us Isaiah 44:3–4: "For I will pour water on the thirsty land, and streams on the dry ground; I will pour out my Spirit on your offspring, and my blessing on your descendants. They will spring up like grass in a meadow, like poplar trees by flowing streams." Through those verses God assured me that He would bring revival among His people and would bless the peoples of the world.

It was more difficult for us to return to America than it had been to go as missionaries to Indonesia, but I felt like Abraham had; I knew that God had spoken. Now it was my turn to obey, even though I could not understand it. I couldn't teach others to obey if I was disobedient. I could not see, as commentator Paul Harvey says, "the rest of the story."

I could not envision hundreds of thousands of persons having their lives changed by God by studying *MasterLife Discipleship Training* and other things I would write in the ensuing years after returning from Indonesia. I could not see the millions whose lives God would transform through studying *Experiencing God: Knowing and Doing the Will of God* that I would help Henry Blackaby publish. I could not see how God would later use my life as I led our missionary work overseas in the role of senior vice president of overseas operations with the International Mission Board.

On the day God encounters us, most of us, like Abraham, cannot envision the part that God wants us to play in His mission. However, God encounters us in a personal experience.

27

God is at work everywhere all the time! When you adjust your life to join Him where He is working, you are dropped into the time line of His global and eternal kingdom activity. In the diagram above, you will observe the process of how God includes you in His mission through a personal encounter.

The arrow in the diagram represents time. God has been at work before you joined Him, and He will be at work after you complete the assignments He gives you during your lifetime. God is moving from eternity to encounter you in time to lead you into eternity. The Seven Realities in the *Experiencing God* diagram, which will be the headings in the first part of this chapter and the following chapters, show how God leads you to obedience. Once God has your ongoing obedience, you are ready to participate in advancing His kingdom purpose. *On Mission with God* is designed to help you make the adjustments needed to join God's mission to the world in this generation.

ABRAHAM'S CLOSE-UP VIEW OF EXPERIENCING GOD THROUGH SEVEN REALITIES

Reality #1: God is always at work around you. We do not know how God appeared personally to Abraham, but it is clear from the beginning that God was going to reveal Himself through His promises. You will notice that God encountered Abraham. It wasn't Abraham who encountered God. At their encounter God promised to bless Abraham if he would obey (Gen. 12:1–8).

As you observe this wandering Bedouin, you may believe that you could never be like Abraham, called "the father of faith" and

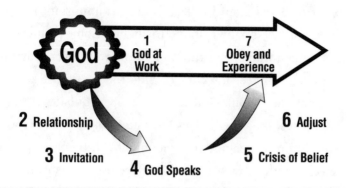

"God's friend" (James 2:23). Yet Abraham started out as a person plagued by persistent fear—the opposite of faith!

Abraham knew that God was at work around him when he encountered Him in Ur of the Chaldees (also known as Mesopotamia, which is in modern Iran). Later in Haran (in modern Syria), where Abraham had stopped with his father on the way to Canaan, God met Abraham and told him to leave everything and go to a distant land.

Abraham was a man riddled with fear. Leaving behind his country, his people, and his father's household would have been a difficult adjustment for him at age seventy-five. Yet by faith Abraham left them all and followed God—not knowing his destination. All he knew was that God promised to make a name for him, bless him, and make him a blessing to all peoples.

Recently I talked with a group of young people who had followed God's call to leave their homes and homelands to join God on mission in His world. I was interested to learn that most of them had thought they were heading for a particular country, only to find that in the process of going, God redirected them to another! They felt a little like Abraham did as he followed God.

In order to be willing to follow God, it is important to understand how you personally respond to change. Some people dislike change so much that they cannot envision any shift occurring in their lives. Others feel insecure outside their comfort zone and perceive that they would fail if they stepped outside of it. Still others don't feel they themselves have anything to offer God and can't even begin to imagine that He might call them to do something special. Others want to think of themselves as available to God, yet they feel uncomfortable relying totally on His strength and not on their own.

None of those attitudes express a true willingness to follow God. God demands obedience. God is at work in you and around you all the time, and He expects you to be ready if He calls you.

Reality #2: God pursues a continuing love relationship with you that is real and personal. When God encountered Abraham to show him how He was working in His world, amazingly, Abraham responded in faith. That was a loving and convincing encounter! Abraham knew he had met God. God initiated a love connection that changed Abraham's heart forever by choosing him out of a pagan culture and calling him to a one-on-one relationship with Himself.

Abraham responded to God's love by building an altar to God at Bethel and worshiping Him (Gen. 12:1–8). As He encountered Abraham, God encounters you every day on His way to redeem the world, and He invites you to join Him. In a life-changing encounter called salvation, God pursued and won your heart. Now that you are a part of His people, He intends to involve you in His mission to the world. He particularly speaks to you when you deeply worship Him, as Abraham did. His encounters are always directed to move you into the flow of His eternal and global kingdom activity. God encounters you every day on His way to redeem the world, and He invites you to join Him.

Reality #3: God invites you to become involved with Him in His work. God's invitation to Abraham involved his descendants, who would be His means to bless the nations. But not long after he arrived in the promised land, Abraham left without consulting God (Gen. 12:10–20). Although Abraham at first believed God's promise about his becoming a great nation, his chronic weakness—fear—almost took away his wife and the mother of the promised son!

Famine sent Abraham scuttling for Egypt, and his fear placed Sarah in jeopardy with Pharaoh. Note that Abraham asked her to say she was his sister (which was a half-truth), to save his own skin. God intervened to salvage the situation, but can you imagine what the Egyptian ruler thought about God after seeing this faithless behavior on Abraham's part?

This story about Abraham's foibles reminds us that God does not expect perfection from us—only obedience and willingness on our part. Some people are so perfectionist that they feel they can never measure up to God's standard, so they don't even try. Others are so aware of their own limitations that they believe God will overlook them. Persons who truly want to follow God are inspired by Abraham's story and realize that God can use them in spite of their weaknesses.

An encounter with God is an opportunity to respond to Him. Prepare to respond by listening carefully to Him. Attune yourself to the ways through which He speaks.

Reality #4: God speaks to you by the Holy Spirit through the Bible, prayer, circumstances, and the church to reveal Himself, His purposes, and His ways. Without the Scriptures, how did Abraham hear from God? We don't know, but from the Bible accounts we can see Abraham clearly knew it was God speaking. One who worships God as Abraham did puts himself or herself in the position to hear from the Lord. Today, as God's child, you have His Holy Spirit residing within you to illuminate the written Word. God will show you His will through His written Word, as you read the Bible or hear it explained. God will speak to you in worship, as you experience Him in praise and worship. God will guide you when you pray, as you experience His presence and love. God will direct you through other people and their testimonies. He may direct you through everyday life experiences of discipline. Never forget, as a Christian, the Holy Spirit resides within you to witness to you. You can be sure that each time God encounters you—however it is—He has a loving purpose to involve you in His work.

Reality #5: God's invitation for you to work with Him always leads you to a crisis of belief that requires faith and action. Even in his fear Abraham was a person of faith and action. We saw how he left his homeland, not knowing where he was going, and gladly replaced stable living with nomadic wanderings. His faith was tested through crises as he was refined to God's standard. Many of the crises were within his own family, as God worked through him to bless his family and through them all peoples.

God was at work in Abraham's life amidst a difficult family situation when his nephew, Lot, chose the best part of the promised land for his home (Gen. 13:5–18). As Lot's herdsmen quarreled with Abraham's herdsmen, the patriarch permitted his nephew to take the most fertile plain. God immediately reassured Abraham that he and his descendants would inherit the whole land.

Families are not perfect, just as individuals are not perfect. That's a reality because of the Fall. Some families, however, are healthier than others, and some are more dysfunctional than others. Yet family dynamics often produce a crisis of faith and impede people from joining God in His work. For example, some people face hostility when they try to tell an unsaved relative about Jesus. They face the burden of trying to maintain good relations despite negative reactions.

In my role with the International Mission Board, I often meet people wanting to follow God's leadership and go overseas as missionaries but who face outright opposition—sometimes hostility—from loved ones who oppose their moving so far away. Sometimes the opposition comes from nonbelieving relatives, but at other times it comes from Christians who have yet to grasp the importance of being open to following God wherever and however He leads. I know a number of missionaries who have followed God rather than succumb to the opposition of relatives. God has blessed because of their decision and many of them have used their commitment to lead family members to Christ.

Reality #6: You must make major adjustments in your life to join God in what He is doing. As Abraham joined God on His mission, he struggled with many major adjustments. At one point this peace-loving patriarch was called on to battle with four kings to rescue his nephew Lot and his family (Gen. 14:11–24). Abraham could have let Lot reap the consequences of his selfish choice to live in Sodom. Instead, he acted immediately, routed the enemy, and recovered all the people and plunder.

Abraham made sure that man's actions would not be cited as the reason for his blessings. He would not take any of the plunder because he wanted the glory to go to God for blessing him. You may have found that human nature rebels against responding immediately to God's directive. Fear, anxiety, comfort, and untold excuses may try to deter you. You discover, however, that when you obey, God blesses beyond measure any adjustments you make to follow Him.

Reality #7: You experience God's purpose as you obey Him and He accomplishes His work through you for His glory. As Abraham gradually learned who God was, his faith grew immeasurably as he obeyed God and saw Him intervene on his behalf. I am most aware of the glory of God's presence when He works through me to accomplish His will. I feel His presence when He leads someone to believe in Him through my witness. God demonstrates His purpose and His glory when He works through us.

In his book on Abraham, Henry notes the importance of obedience in the lives of biblical figures such as Abraham and the disciples of Jesus. He notes that except for Judas, no disciples showed any sign of rebellion (John 17:12). "There is sin in other areas of their lives, but one does not see an attitude of wanting to do the wrong thing. They may fail, but not out of rebellion or hardness of heart. They had to learn the hard way often, but God was present to forgive, guide, and encourage them. They always responded in loving faith and continued obedience!"[1]

As you finish looking at the Seven Realities of Experiencing God in Abraham's life, evaluate where you are personally in the process. Which step are you on, and what is holding you back from moving on to the next reality? Identify anything you think God sees in your heart that could hold you back from obeying Him (Ps. 139:23–24).

THE WIDE-ANGLE PERSPECTIVE OF GOD ENCOUNTERING ABRAHAM THROUGH A LIFETIME OF PERSONAL EXPERIENCES

We have now explored the *Experiencing God* picture—how God works with us through initial experiences using the Seven Realities. But that is a limited view. Now we need to back up for a wide-angle perspective and see what God was doing through Abraham's lifetime of experiencing God. We will track the Seven Spiritual Markers that God uses with His people. We will see how the Lord chooses us, calls us, covenants with us, prepares us, sends us, guides us, and uses us to accomplish His mission that the glory of God will cover the earth.

Abraham's First Spiritual Marker: God's Choice. God's purpose in choosing Abraham wasn't merely to bless him but to make him a blessing to all nations. When God comes to you, He has a much bigger picture than your personal salvation in mind. He has chosen you to be involved in His worldwide kingdom for the rest of your life.

If you know Him, you realize that God chose you to be His child. He cared enough about you to find you. He encountered you to show you His love and brought you to a crisis of belief where you trusted Him, made the adjustment to follow Him, and obeyed Him. Why did God do that? Because He sees you as a part

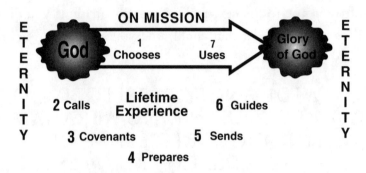

of what He will do in the world during your generation! Can you identify any indications that God wants to use you in His larger purpose in the world?

Abraham's Second Spiritual Marker: God's Call. God calls you just as He called Abraham. You may say, "I enjoy an intimate relationship with God, but I'm not called to be a preacher." Abraham wasn't a preacher, either. God called Abraham because He wanted to call a people to Himself. Once God called him, He began to speak to him, and Abraham began to understand that God's mission for him was larger than he could imagine.

When God tells you to follow Him, He is not obligated to reveal your destination immediately. I did not know where God wanted me to serve until eleven years after I answered God's call to be on mission with Him overseas. I visited numerous countries, but God did not tell me that any of those places was where I was to go. Just before we were to be appointed as missionaries, the Lord revealed it was Indonesia. If you follow Him in faith, He will lead you to the place where He can best use you. Hebrews 11:6 says, "Now without faith it is impossible to please God, for the one who draws near to Him must believe that He exists and rewards those who seek Him." You obey by faith!

Abraham's Third Spiritual Marker: God's covenant and promised blessings. Abraham discovered that God loves to create, to bless, and to redeem. He not only chooses and calls, but He also makes a covenant with you, just as He did with Abraham (Gen. 12:1–3). This is the first covenant He made with Abraham, regarding the blessing of the nations.

Notice that God's blessing included His promises, but with every blessing comes a responsibility. If you experience only the blessing, you're only halfway there! For every top-line blessing a bottom-line responsibility exists. How has God blessed you, and in what ways is He using you to bless others?

In Genesis 15, God repeated His promise to Abraham in a way he could not forget. Abraham complained that he didn't have a son and that his servant would have to receive his inheritance. God promised that Abraham would have a son and gave him an object lesson (Gen. 15:4–6). When God makes a promise, He gives His word that it will come to pass. As Abraham surveyed the eastern sky, he experienced God's glory. Approximately six thousand stars are visible to the naked eye, but God's promise went far beyond anything Abraham could imagine—Abraham's descendants would be as uncountable as the stars. God's glory is manifest in the greatness of His promises (Eph. 3:20).

Next Abraham experienced God's covenant in a vivid way. This occurred when God told Abraham to do something, and Abraham responded (Gen. 15:9–18). As the sun set, Abraham fell into a deep sleep, almost like a coma. In his vision God told him to bring a heifer, a goat, and a ram to sacrifice. Abraham cut the animals in half and arranged the halves across from each other.

In this vision God and Abraham "cut a covenant." In Abraham's culture and time, two people entered into a binding agreement as they "cut a covenant." This made the agreement binding on both parties. To do this they walked between the two halves of sacrificed animals. In this vision Abraham saw a smoking firepot with a blazing torch appear and pass through the cut animals. God had walked between the sacrificed animals and "cut a covenant" with Abraham.

God, not you, initiates covenants. Making a covenant with God is much more serious than you may realize. Your covenant with Him is your response to His initiative. God promises you many things, but each depends on your obedience to Him. God tells you what He will do if you obey! When God makes a covenant, He keeps His word, and He expects you to keep yours! Has God made any promises to you? If so, do you know what your part of the covenant is? Keep in mind that God's plan for your life involves your believing His promise to you as you experience Him on mission.

Abraham's Fourth Spiritual Marker: God prepares him for His mission. It took God twenty-five years to shape Abraham's character to the point where he could be the father Isaac needed. During that time God dealt with Abraham's greatest weakness—fear. Even though he believed God's promise about an heir, Abraham's fear fed on Sarah's continuing childlessness. God had a lot of work to do with Sarah as well before she could become the mother God wanted her to be. Sarah blamed God for her barrenness and turned to her maidservant to provide an heir, then later blamed Hagar for her sufferings (Gen. 16:1–5). Before God was finished with Abraham and Sarah, He would transform their faithlessness and fearfulness into faithfulness and fearlessness. Meanwhile God was grinding them, testing them, and allowing them to get into problems that He would use to transform their character.

When you have troubles, recognize that God is shaping you and molding you for His purpose. At one time a dazzling diamond was merely a piece of black coal. With pressure, time, and cutting, it became a beautiful jewel! The grand design for diamonds in God's kingdom is that all the peoples of the world will be blessed through His people, including you! What rough edges in your character is God working on in order to use you to the maximum on mission with Him?

Abraham's Fifth Spiritual Marker: God sends him to the place where He can best work through him to accomplish His mission. The delightful day finally arrived when Isaac, the child of promise, was born into Abraham's household. For a quarter of a century, through tough times of testing, Abraham finally matured into the father of faith. Abraham and Sarah must have thought they were "home free" in their faith walk with God. In Genesis 17, Abraham obeyed God immediately when He introduced the covenant of circumcision. In Genesis 21:11–14, the distressed patriarch submitted to God in sending away his other son, Ishmael. Abraham must have hoped that his trials were over. But the worst—and biggest—test was yet to occur. God was getting ready to send Abraham on a journey that would cut him to his very core (Gen. 22:1–18).

What must have run through Abraham's mind when God sent him on this harrowing expedition! I can just imagine him saying something like, "But God, I'm over one hundred years old. My heart won't take these shocks. You gave me this child. The heathen do these abominable things like human sacrifice. How can this possibly glorify You?" But Abraham had heard the voice of God often enough to know it was God speaking. Early the next day he set out on his sad journey. Knowing that Isaac was his only hope for name, inheritance, and blessing to all peoples, Abraham trusted that God would raise Isaac from the dead, if necessary (Heb. 11:19). He believed God and hoped in Him.

Can you recall a time when God brought you through some physical or emotional experience—a time when He was your only hope? If you can, you know that a loving Father's grace is sufficient in your weakness (2 Cor. 12:9).

Abraham's Sixth Spiritual Marker: God guides him on mission with Him. Abraham could not have envisioned the great mission and the glory God would receive from it as he prepared to sacrifice the son of promise. From the very outset, however, God knew that He would have to guide Abraham unerringly to carefully foreshadow the giving up of His only begotten Son years later. In fact, the showdown came on the very mountain, Moriah, where Christ would be crucified! (Gen. 22:1–12).

God not only guided him to the right mountain (Gen. 22:2) but also provided Abraham with prophetic words to answer his son's question, "God himself will provide the lamb for the burnt offering (Gen. 22:8). God intervened at the crucial moment to prevent Abraham from plunging the knife into his son's heart (Gen. 22:10–12). Finally, the One whom Abraham called "the LORD

40

will provide" showed him the ram caught in the thicket—the sacrifice that would take the place of Isaac (Gen. 22:13). The happy ending occurred when God provided the ram and made Isaac the answer to Abraham's hope. The patriarch had finally moved from fear to faith that God would fulfill His promises!

Think about your own faith encounters with God. Compare how God met you with the way He spoke to and answered Abraham. If God has not yet led you through such an experience, ask Him to guide you to one.

I work with five thousand missionaries who, like Abraham, left their home, family, and friends. Seldom do they mention their deprivations. More often they say, "This is great. I'm doing what God wants me to do. I enjoy living here. What a privilege to see God work!" God calls each of us to present our bodies "a living sacrifice, holy and pleasing to God; this is your spiritual worship" (Rom. 12:1). Such sacrifices bring a "soothing aroma" to Him (Lev. 1:13, 17 NASB). Your sacrifice of yourself on a daily basis will guarantee that you will experience Him through His daily guidance in your life!

Abraham's Seventh Spiritual Marker: God uses him to bring glory to His name as He accomplishes His mission through him. From studying these incidents with Abraham, you realize that everything begins with God and not with you. Sometimes you may think you have a better idea and want to bargain with God: "If You'll make this happen, I'll serve You. If You'll bless this business, I'll give You a tithe or offering." This is the opposite of what God does. He covenants with you and tells you what He will do in and for and through you, as He did with Abraham.

Sometimes I have not been as quick to obey as Abraham was. When God first spoke to me at a youth rally and impressed me about missions, I responded, "I don't want to live in a grass hut in Africa! I'm comfortable here in America." However, the Holy Spirit moved me to respond to the invitation. The person who counseled me didn't report that I surrendered to be a missionary—only that I had been called to preach. Because of that, I rationalized that I didn't "have to go," but God continued to call me.

I finally tried to bargain with God. I told Him, "If I marry a girl who is going to be a missionary, then I'll be one, too." Now that was a bold decision, wasn't it? Actually, God got it settled before I started dating her. But when I finally surrendered to be a missionary, God spoke to me, saying, "Be an evangelist!" I responded, "But, God, now I want to go." He said, "Be an evangelist." I replied, "But I really want to go be a missionary." God said, "You'll go someday, but now I want you to be an evangelist." For the next eleven years, I did evangelism and was pastor of three churches before He let me go to another land as a "field evangelist." As I write this many years later, it just occurred to me that God was telling me what I was to do at that point in my life rather than where I was to do it!

If you have struggled with a call from God and you still feel Him calling you, obey. God can still use you to accomplish His mission. Whether His call is to another people or to your own people, God is working to lead you to join His mission. If you don't respond to God to be on mission with Him, you will miss experiencing God's glory through your life.

You may not realize why you, like Abraham, have undergone trials and testing. Abraham's experience should encourage you. These testing times could be God's indications that He has a significant assignment for you. God is using them to shape you into His image and prepare you to be on mission with Him. God cares enough to work in you and through you to accomplish His mission in the world (Phil. 2:13; 4:4–6).

ABRAHAM'S 180-DEGREE CORPORATE EXPERIENCE WITH THE SPIRITUAL MARKERS

When God chose Abraham, He had in mind a much greater purpose than saving one individual. God's mission was to make Abraham into a great nation to bless all peoples on the face of the earth. His covenant with Abraham was confirmed with his son Isaac (Gen. 26:13; 28:10–15). God used the same Seven Spiritual Markers with his corporate people that He used with Abraham.

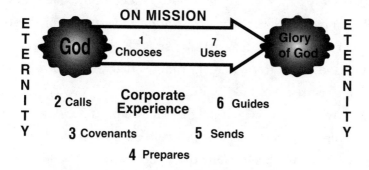

Corporate Spiritual Marker #1: God chooses each generation of His people to bless all nations. Throughout Scripture you see that God continued to bless Abraham's descendants until they became the great nation of Israel, numbering in the millions. Hosea prophesied that the Israelites would be like the sand on the seashore and would be called "sons of the living God" (Hos. 1:10).

God always had the big picture in mind, seeing generations into the future when all nations would be blessed by Abraham's seed (singular), meaning Christ (Gal. 3:16). In Galatians 3:14, Paul states clearly, "The purpose was that the blessing of Abraham would come to the Gentiles in Christ Jesus, so that we could receive the promise of the Spirit through faith." Notice that God's plan in choosing Abraham encompassed the coming of Christ, the promise of the Holy Spirit, and salvation for Gentiles as well as Jews.

When God chose you, what did He have in mind? You might be as surprised as Abraham to see the fulfillment of God's promises. Have you been praying for your descendants? When Shirley and I faced the decision I mentioned at the beginning of this chapter, she said, "Look at the next verse, Isaiah 44:3, which says, 'I will pour out my Spirit on your offspring and my blessing on your descendants.' We need to ask for some Bible promises for our kids." God led us to two other promises that we claimed for our five children (Isa. 58:11–12; 59:21).

We have the promise of God that He will bless our descendants for all time! I wish I had space to tell you how God has blessed our descendants already. Our five children are all walking with Jesus and serving Him—two of them in church-related vocations. They are training our thirteen grandchildren to follow Christ. Henry and Marilynn Blackaby have claimed Bible promises for their five children, too, and all five of them are in ministry or missions, and they are praying for their thirteen grandchildren to be on mission with God.

Has God given you promises for your descendants? If not, begin now to ask God to give you Scriptures that you can claim for your physical or spiritual children as you study *On Mission with God*.

Corporate Spiritual Marker #2: God calls your generation to Himself to be on mission with Him. God knew when He called us that leaving us on our own to do His mission would not be a good idea. Instead, He put His Holy Spirit within us and made us members of Christ's body (Eph. 5:30).

Just as God chose Israel to be His special people in the Old Testament, He has "called out" the church to be its New Testament counterpart. The Lord designed the church to be a multifaceted group with varying gifts (Rom. 12:4–6a; 1 Cor. 12:12, 14, 18, 27). The New Testament Greek word for *church* is *ekklesia*, which means "called out."

As part of the body of Christ, you have an interdependent relationship with people of like mind and heart whose spiritual gifts complement one another. Through worship and the Word, God works in and through His church so that, together with other members, you accomplish His mission in the world. In this generation the Lord is bringing a new unity and harmony to bear in His body so He can reach the world through us.

God has called you to pursue unity in His church and to work harmoniously with your brothers and sisters in Christ (John 17:16–23). Only then will His glory rest on you as you, in partnership with others in the body of Christ, seek to join Him on mission.

Corporate Spiritual Marker #3: God initiates a covenant of promise and obedience with your generation. In *The Experiencing God Study Bible,* Henry defines the church in a way that emphasizes this covenant relationship with God. He says, "The church is the body of people God has chosen to enter into a love relationship with Him through faith in Jesus Christ as Lord and Savior, having committed themselves to obey Him and join the work He is doing. God's chosen people, Israel, was the precursor or forerunner of the church, only a faithful remnant serving as God's people."[2]

Although God chose a single individual to begin a nation, His purpose is to bring together a covenant people who will gather representatives from every nation, tribe, tongue, and people to bring glory to Him throughout eternity (1 Pet. 2:9–10). Today, when so much emphasis is placed on individuality, you may find it hard to understand how God works with His people corporately. Know that God's purpose for the people of this world is so great that it will take all His people to reach them.

Corporate Spiritual Marker #4: God is preparing this generation of His people for His mission. You may believe that life is much more difficult for you than it was for previous generations. However, Abraham and other Bible heroes clearly encountered many struggles in following God. Some in the generations just before you suffered through two world wars and left homes and families to fight against earthly foes. Paul said to Timothy, a young person of his generation, "Share in suffering as a good soldier of Christ Jesus" (2 Tim. 2:3). God is giving this generation a great deal of on-the-job training and character-building opportunities as He prepares His people for His heavenly purpose in these end times!

I see many heartbreaking situations among the people of God all over the world. Christian believers have their homes ransacked or are arrested and interrogated. Some are imprisoned. Others, such as Chu Hon Yi and his wife Kei Yi, have been martyred in recent years. They form a modern catalog of heroes, such as those in Hebrews 11. Times have not changed much, when you look at the whole world.

You have probably noticed the difference between what happened to the people described in Hebrews 11:1–34 and those mentioned in verses 35–38. People in the latter group suffered persecution and death for their faith. Note that both groups were commended for their faith, but none have yet received the promise. The writer of Hebrews says that God planned something better for us so that only together with us would they be made perfect! That "large cloud of witnesses" (Heb. 12:1) is looking over the banisters of heaven, urging Christ's church on to final victory. Time is running out. I am impressed with today's younger generation, which is ready to go wherever God is on mission. In our day, that is literally to the ends of the earth!

Corporate Spiritual Marker #5: God is sending this generation of His people to the places where He can best work through them to accomplish His mission. Throughout history God has moved people from one place to another for His purposes. You have seen how Abraham had to travel long distances to be in the place of God's choosing for Him. Similarly, seventy members of the family of Jacob went down into Egypt where God would make of them a great nation (Exod. 1:1). Some four hundred years later

He brought them out of Egypt into Canaan. Later they were taken captive to Babylon and returned to Palestine after seventy years of captivity (Jer. 25:8–14). In the New Testament the disciples were scattered after the stoning of Stephen (Acts 8:1–4). The destruction of Jerusalem in A.D. 70 dispersed God's people throughout the Roman world. When you look at all of history, it seems that God has always had His people on the move.

Have you ever stopped to think about how many persons in your church have traveled out of your country on business or pleasure in the last three years alone? I would expect that number to be fairly large. Additionally, have you ever stopped to calculate how many from your church have gone on mission trips just in the past three years? And how many missionaries have been called from your church and live outside the country now? And how many business or professional people or students from your church are now living abroad?

All over the world, people are traveling to different cultures and actually moving from one country to another, from one continent to another. Have you ever wondered why this is happening? One of the results is that this movement is literally making it possible for your church and almost every other church to become a world-missions strategy center to commission people to be on mission with God.

Throughout the Bible you see how God has chosen a people and prepared them to be His representatives, His ambassadors, and His reconcilers in the world. He wants your church to be involved! As you go about your church and worship activities, be observant of any indications where you see God working in new ways to involve your church in His mission.

Corporate Spiritual Marker #6: God is guiding His people in this generation to be on mission with Him.

Since it is God's mission, He takes total responsibility for guiding a willing group of people to the proper destination. God guided Abraham in the midst of His activity to get him to the right place at the right time. God is able to guide His people at any given time, and He is no less interested in this generation than in any other.

More than two hundred years ago, Adoniram Judson and Luther Rice heard God's call and left America to go to India as missionaries from the Congregational Church. On the trip overseas they studied their Bibles and decided to be immersed as Baptists. Upon their arrival William Carey baptized them. They were not allowed to serve in India, so Judson and his wife, Ann, went to Burma. Since their support would no longer come from the Congregationalists, Rice returned to America to raise money. Out of his efforts came the Triennial Baptist Convention, the precursor to the American Baptist Churches and the Southern Baptist Convention.

Meanwhile, Judson served six years before he saw his first convert. I visited Myanmar (Burma) in 1999. The Baptist Convention of Myanmar has 700,000 members divided into fifteen people-group conventions. Judson could not have imagined that he would be a blessing to so many peoples! Rice could never have imagined that one of the conventions (the Southern Baptist Convention) that he helped start would become the largest missionary-sending denomination in the world. Like Abraham and Sarah, Judson and Rice acted on faith.

Read the parable of the landowner and his vineyard in Matthew 20:1–16. This parable is a picture of God. The Prime Mover is making sure the harvest is gathered. The Scriptures record God's activity. Whether you work with internationals around your church or go overseas as a volunteer or a short-term or career missionary, you can know that the God who guided you there will reveal the assignments He has for you. Also pray for your fellow laborers that have been sent to gather in the harvest.

Corporate Spiritual Marker #7: God is using this generation to fulfill His mission. God has designed us to function as a people united with one heart and mind. Like it or not, your life is linked with others by God's design. One of the great moves of God in this generation is to help people understand the value of corporate life among churches, associations, denominations, and Christian organizations as part of His kingdom. In what ways is your church involved with other Christians in reaching the world for Christ?

THE 360-DEGREE ETERNAL PERSPECTIVE

Being on mission with God is much like climbing a mountain. As you climb, you begin to see the peak of the mountain looming before you that represents your experience with God. What a blessing this close-up experience with God is as you join Him on mission through the Seven Realities and get to know Him better. But that experience is surpassed as you reach the top of the mountain and realize that God is giving you a wide-angle view of the whole mountain—your whole lifetime guided by Seven Spiritual Markers. Then as the mist evaporates, you look around to see a

180-degree view of your life influencing God's people to be on mission with Him. But one day God will lift you up to see a 360-degree view of the whole mountain range and your part in His eternal purpose. God used Abraham to show us three revelations of His eternal purpose.

Eternal Revelation #1: God's blessings come to us to move through us. God loves to bless. One of the first times God blesses in Scripture occurs when He made people in His image and likeness. "God blessed them and said to them, 'Be fruitful and increase in number; fill the earth and subdue it. Rule over the fish of the sea and the birds of the air and over every living creature that moves on the ground'" (Gen. 1:28). Obviously God's blessings came to Adam and Eve to move through them to bless the entire creation. Today God desires to do the same through you!

My close friend, Tom Elliff, taught me a new definition of *blessing*. "In the biblical sense a 'blessing' is an act of God by which He causes someone or something to supernaturally produce more than would be naturally possible." He said, "When you ask the Lord, for instance, to bless a certain missionary, you are asking God to give him the ability to accomplish more than is humanly possible. Praying that God bless an offering indicates a desire for God to superintend the use of that money so that it accomplishes more than it would if dispensed on the basis of human cleverness."[3] God desires to bless you by making you fruitful "in every good work" (Col. 1:10) and watching you increase in faith (2 Cor. 10:15). He desires that through you the knowledge of His glory will increase and fill the whole earth (Hab. 2:14). He wants you to walk in His authority as you go and disciple all nations (Matt. 28:18–19) and subdue the kingdom of

51

darkness (Rom. 16:20) so that you may rule and reign with Him in His kingdom (Rev. 5:10).

Although God began His creation by blessing Adam and Eve in the garden of Eden, the primary revelation of God's desire to bless all nations is demonstrated through Abraham. As part of God's covenant of blessing with Abraham, He prospered him physically and spiritually in everything he did. God blessed him with great wealth and flocks and herds (Gen. 13:2). Abraham had so many physical blessings that he and his nephew Lot parted company because the land could not support all their possessions (Gen. 13:6).

Scripture indicates that the patriarchs blessed their children as they placed their hands on their heads. This blessing was based on the fact that God had blessed them, and this was an affirmation of God's blessings to their offspring. Certainly the fathers bequeathed physical blessings to their offspring, especially the firstborn. The inheritance included the idea that the spiritual blessings from God overshadowed them and would continue through the generations. Even today the idea of a blessing by one's parents is important, though it is seldom formal. Sometimes parental approval while the person is alive is more important psychologically than is the actual physical inheritance.

God promised that His blessing would be extended to all peoples of the world through Abraham and His descendants. In fact, God continues to bless anyone connected with Abraham, right down to the present time! That includes you, if you are a believer. Galatians 3:7 tells you that "those who have faith are Abraham's sons." The blessings to Abraham, your spiritual forefather, are designed to flow to you and to bless the nations of the world through you.

Eternal Revelation #2: God's blessings are based on obedience. As you've already studied, God chose Abraham, knowing he would obey Him. God says as much in Genesis 18:19. Note that God's blessing hinged on Abraham's obedience. Disobedience could bring a curse—the opposite of blessing—as it did to Adam and Eve (Gen. 3:14–23), to Noah's generation (Gen. 6), and to Babel (Gen. 11).

God's promise to Abraham included his posterity, the land, and the blessing. God blessed Abraham abundantly for leaving his family and friends to establish the family of nations the Lord desired to bless through him! God's call to Christians to reach the nations will result in rich rewards of relationships enduring into eternity! (Mark 10:29–30).

The promised land was a part of the blessing God gave to Abraham. His willingness to leave Ur, a great cultural center of the day, to wander throughout foreign countries was a real step of faith for him. Several times during Abraham's lifetime, God confirmed the call to Canaan—in Haran, where he settled until his father's death; after he parted from Lot; and after the victorious battle with the kings (Gen. 12:7; 13:14–15; 15:7).

Interestingly, the only part of the promised land that Abraham possessed during his lifetime was the cave of Machpelah, which he purchased to bury Sarah. It was a token of the promise, which would later be fulfilled to the nation that Abraham fathered (Heb. 11:9–10).

You may or may not own a home in the place where you currently live. God may ask you, like Abraham, to leave your homeland and live in a temporary dwelling anywhere in the world. If He does, you will join the ranks of those whose hope rested in God—the founder of an eternal city. There, throughout eternity, you will no longer be a stranger or a foreigner but a child of the king and a citizen of the heavenly kingdom!

The third part of the promise was the blessing itself (Gen. 12:2–3). The word *bless* occurs five times in these verses. When God first called Abraham, God informed him that he was about to be blessed in ways Abraham would see in his lifetime and in ways Abraham was unable to foresee or even remotely understand. Not only was Abraham blessed, but also he would become the means of blessing all peoples on earth. Blessing is never just for you; it is always to be passed on to others! Obedience is the key to eternal blessings.

Eternal Revelation #3: God's promised blessings to those who believe are as sure as the promises He has already fulfilled. The mission to bless all the peoples of the world is a mission to bring all peoples into the family of God. God is not interested in blessing your life merely so you will prosper. The final scene of history is not a throng of individuals standing before the throne recounting their blessings, one by one. Rather, it is a scene of all the people of God—a people drawn from every tribe, language, and people—giving honor and glory to the rightful Lord of all! (Rev. 7:9–10).

Remember the diagram that symbolizes this study? God's promise of blessing on your life is not the target. Look at the target to which the arrow points—the glory of God. In order to join God on mission, always keep in view His target. He is on His way to the world. He initiates encounters with you so that you may join Him, not so that He can join you.

How have you experienced this flow of God's life and message through your own life? You can see from the chart that God has been lifting you into the flow of His kingdom work. Often, when you feel overwhelmed by the problems around you, God has strategically placed you there to advance His kingdom. You may be the only person in a situation who can pray or give godly wisdom or laugh with hope that comes from deep inside. God has connected His life to yours because He wants His "family life" extended to places where only you can take it.

Some four thousand years ago God gave Abraham the promise that all peoples on earth would be blessed through him. Yet, today, approximately two thousand distinct peoples, numbering some 1.7 billion, have no significant number of believers in their midst and have never heard of God's promises of salvation.

For various reasons the 1.7 billion individuals represented by these groups are still unreached with the gospel. Here are some of the reasons:

- Satan does not want redemption to come to them and uses political or religious gatekeepers to keep Christians away from them;
- Satan blinds believers to the big picture, so he is free to reign over vast areas of the earth; and
- Believers get too busy passing the blessings back and forth to one another to consider why God has blessed them in the first place.

You cannot underestimate the spiritual battle that underlies God's mission. Every people without a church is a people whom Satan has locked in captivity. He will not easily give up these people. He will blind believers to God's mission. He will convince you that God is more concerned about you and your people than He is about them.

Ultimately God is shaping your life so that you can join Him on mission. When you align your life with His purpose, you can live with hope and significance. You can be involved in helping to extend the kingdom of God to the ends of the earth through ways such as the following:

- Intercessory prayer;
- Working in your community to help the poor and oppressed so that God's name won't be profaned among the nations;
- Working toward racial reconciliation, as a business person;
- Giving to missions and missionaries;
- Joining a volunteer mission trip;
- Serving in student missions;
- Praying for persecuted Christians;
- Doing a short-term mission assignment;
- Teaching mission education programs in your church;
- Befriending internationals, such as students, in your community; and
- Working in a foreign country and bearing witness to Christ.

You may think of other ways you have already been involved in global purposes or ways you would like to be involved. Ask God to help you see the ways you can join Him in blessing the nations!

Spend some time praying and reflecting on what God has been impressing on your heart as you read this chapter. Then pray one of the following two statements that most reflects where you are right now:

Yes, Lord, I am willing to look among the nations. I want to know what You are doing, and I want to be a part of it. Help me to see the ways You have connected my life to Your mission to glorify Your name among all the peoples of the world.

Yes, Lord, I am willing, but I confess I am still not convinced that this "whole world" thing has anything to do with me. Help me understand how Your mission to bless all peoples of the world connects to my life.

3

MOSES ON MISSION WITH GOD

A PEOPLE RESPONSIBLE FOR ALL PEOPLES

"'My name will be great among the nations,
from the rising to the setting of the sun. In every place
incense and pure offerings will be brought to my
name, because my name will be great among the
nations,' says the LORD Almighty."
—Malachi 1:11

HAVE YOU EVER BEEN IN AN OBSCURE, SEEMINGLY FORSAKEN PLACE
and wondered whether God had forgotten you? Henry felt that
way when he was pastor of the faithless, twelve-member Faith
Baptist Church, of Saskatoon, Saskatchewan, Canada.

This ostensibly unpromising pastorate capped a varied career
for Henry. In his life he had also been an oiler on a one-ton
loraine clam bucket, a deckhand on a coast steamer, in sales for a
gas company, and had worked for Coca-Cola. His father was a

lay preacher-banker who started churches in the fishing villages of British Colombia. After God called him to preach, Henry moved to San Francisco to attend seminary, where he also served as a music director and then as pastor of a small church in nearby San Pablo. After graduation he was pastor of the First Southern Baptist Church of Downey in East Los Angeles. Six years later Faith Baptist Church in Saskatoon called him to be its pastor. The handful of members left in this declining church threatened to disband if he did not accept their invitation. The only thing attractive about this opportunity was God. Faith became a laboratory for *Experiencing God* as Henry served for twelve years in this out-of-the-way place. Along with others, Henry experienced God working in special ways in the Saskatoon revival. It may have been an obscure place, but God knew where Henry was and shaped him there.

As He did with Henry, God knows your address, too. He is at work in your life and has you in the place He wants you. He may not have you in a "whale of a belly" like Jonah or imprisoned like Paul, but wherever you are, He is speaking to you about His mission for your life.

In chapter 2, you learned that obeying God's bidding moves you into the flow of God's glory as He fulfills His promises. God promised a blessing through Abraham for all the peoples of the world, and Abraham responded in obedience. In this chapter you'll see how God moved Moses into His mission and how God plans for His blessings to flow through His people to all people.

Much more occurred than most people realize in Moses' encounter with God in the burning bush (Exod. 3:1–22). God showed His glory in the flames of a bush that did not burn up. God also called Moses by name and then revealed His name. God revealed His character to Moses. He manifested His presence to Moses. And God revealed His purpose for His people.

God called Moses at the burning bush, but He had been shaping Moses for eighty years. God not only saved Moses' life as a baby, He also provided for Moses to learn Hebrew history and culture. He allowed him to participate in the best schooling available in the world while he watched the ins and outs of the great nation of Egypt. Moses had to flee Pharaoh's court and spend forty years on the backside of the desert after he tried to begin an Israelite revolution. But God had not forgotten him. Moses was gaining personal knowledge of every trail, well, and mountain in the desert of Midian and Sinai—experiences he would need later to lead the Israelites to freedom in the promised land.

God also prepares you for your part in His mission by encountering you in various ways. When you join God on mission, He reveals His presence to you in your daily life, and your life is linked to His eternal certainty. God interacts with you daily, because He is personally concerned for you.

You may be involved in an incredibly painful personal experience or family trouble. You may wonder what your life has to do with God's mission. The Israelites in Egypt thought the same thing before Moses arrived!

God had been working long before Moses, just as He had been in Abraham's time. In fact, when the children of Israel were just getting started on their 430-year sojourn in Egypt, Joseph had prophesied: "But God will surely come to your aid and take you up out of this land to the land he promised on oath to Abraham, Isaac and Jacob" (Gen. 50:24). Little did Moses know that centuries later, God had planned to get glory by tapping him to be the leader in this momentous event that would fulfill His promise.

MOSES' CLOSE-UP VIEW OF THE SEVEN REALITIES OF EXPERIENCING GOD

Reality #1: God is always at work around you. God was working at the time of Moses' birth to prepare him for His mission. Although Moses was born into slavery, God saw to it that he was rescued and reared by Pharaoh's daughter as well as by his own Hebrew mother. The Lord even worked through the Egyptian princess to name him (Exod. 2:10). Moses means "drawn out." I wonder if God influenced this name selection because Moses also would draw out the children of Israel to follow God in the wilderness. Moses had the best of both worlds—Egyptian culture and education together with Hebrew devotion to God. From his Levite parents he had heard the story of how God worked among His people and the promises of how He would use Abraham's descendants to bless all peoples of the world!

Some people mistakenly believe God is at work in their lives because He wants to give them a purpose. The truth is God is at work in your life because He has an eternal mission and wants to uniquely involve you in His purpose. God shapes you, just as He was shaping Moses, to be a part of His mission.

Reality #2: God pursues a continuing love relationship with you that is real and personal. As Moses grew up in Pharaoh's palace, perhaps he questioned, as you might have at some point, "Why am I here? Does God even know that I am here? And why is it so difficult for me to find my place in His plan?" Moses had been told the stories of his forefathers. He must have wondered if the God who had a personal relationship with Abraham had any interest in him.

Perhaps the Israelites were hoping the Hebrew prince in the palace would resolve their plight. Moses probably saw himself as their deliverer. When he was grown, he took a walk among his people and intervened for their sake (Exod. 2:11–12). He felt a connection—an ethnic identity—with the Hebrews, "his own people." We do know from the biblical account that Moses saw the Hebrews working at hard labor—prisoner-slaves forced to do the impossible with meager supplies—and he saw a cruel Egyptian taskmaster beat one of these Hebrew slaves. We also know he saw God's covenant with Abraham being mocked by the captivity of God's people.

The cruelty, suffering, and injustice of the Egyptian oppression probably overwhelmed Moses. He identified with the Egyptian Pharaoh through adoption by Pharaoh's daughter. On the other hand, in his formative years his mother-nurse taught him that he was a Hebrew. He may have made the connection that he had come to the kingdom for such a time as this. He made a conscious decision to throw in his lot with the despised slaves rather than enjoy the pleasures of sin for a season (Heb. 11:24–25). Moses took things into his own hands. Encountering an Egyptian abusing an Israelite slave, he intervened and killed the Egyptian. He may have thought that Israel would respond to his revolutionary act, follow him, and win freedom from Egyptian bondage. But when he tried to make peace between two quarreling Israelites, their response showed that others knew that he murdered the Egyptian. He fled to the desert in Midian for the next forty years!

As you and I have done, Moses attempted to do God's work by himself. When he failed, he ran from the responsibility that

God wanted to give him. Later, this weakness exerted itself again when Moses complained that the people weren't following him. Even near his life's end, this weakness caused him to disobey God and kept him from entering the promised land.

Have you ever felt, like Moses, that a situation is intolerable and that something must be done? Did you sense you should do something or that God was up to something? In fact, God was grabbing your attention. The most important thing in Moses' life, both on the day he murdered the Egyptian and for the next forty years he would spend in hiding, was surely the plight of the Israelite people and his role in their cause. Do you believe God will use events and people around you to open your eyes to what He is determined to accomplish?

One way to recognize that God is laying the needs of the world on your heart is to become aware of your own responses when you hear about troubles that the world's lost, distraught, suffering people are experiencing.

Reality #3: God invites you to become involved with Him in His work. God encounters you because He is on His way to a well-defined end. He wants to involve you in what He is about to do (Exod. 3:1–10).

Just as in your encounters with God, when Moses met God that day, it was not at Moses' initiative. As incredibly intriguing as Moses' life had been up to that point, it wasn't Moses who decided it was time to intervene in Middle Eastern history for the sake of the kingdom of God. On that fateful day in the desert, when God and Moses met over a burning bush, both had a history. The story of Moses up to that day is one of great drama—the reed-basket bobbing in the Nile, the young Jewish slave boy morphing into a stately Egyptian prince, the hotheaded young man murdering his way into a desert oblivion. You could easily be tempted to misread the exodus story as Moses' encounter with God.

However, the God who is always achieving His unchanging purpose brought to that burning bush an even more compelling drama. Using a reluctant Egyptian Pharaoh and a remarkably storied man named Moses, God was about to reveal just how intent He was in making His purpose known! As you read Moses' story, ask if God is working to get your attention to involve you in His mission.

Reality #4: God speaks to you by the Holy Spirit through the Bible, prayer, circumstances, and the church to reveal Himself, His purposes, and His ways. Although God speaks to His people in many ways, He used a burning bush only once! I wonder what would have happened if Moses hadn't gone over to look. When Moses did, God spoke to him. When Moses answered the burning-bush call that day, God had more in mind than freeing the Hebrew slaves—even though their plight surely deserved His attention. He was on mission—a mission that stretched back to a promise made to Abraham some 430 years earlier (Gen. 15:13–18; Exod. 3:6). The bush was not burning to invite Moses to help free the Hebrew slaves. It was burning to issue an invitation for Moses to join God on the mission that God had declared to Abraham. God's purpose has never changed! His mission is no different today than it was fifty years ago or twenty-five hundred years ago. It does not differ from individual to individual or from church to church or from nation to nation.

God speaks by the Holy Spirit through the Word of God and prayer and circumstances that are interpreted by the body of Christ. God speaks, and yet each of us in different ways perceives how God speaks to us. In the Bible God is always speaking. As you go through the Word, you read, "the Lord said," "God said," and "thus saith the Lord." Interestingly, no matter how He spoke to people in the Bible, the one thing they always knew was that it was God. They understood who was speaking, and they knew what He was saying. The story of Moses contains no equivocation. He knew what God was saying; he just didn't want to do it. God speaks to you uniquely, but He's always speaking. He's always showing you His purpose and inviting you to experience His glory. He wants to involve you in what He's doing.

God Himself made an oath because God is determined to make His purpose clear and to show that it is unchanging (Heb. 6:17). From this verse, you can see that God's mission—His driving purpose—is consistent throughout the Bible and throughout history to show His glory to all peoples. To understand exactly what God is doing in your world today, come back to this central point: He is determined to fulfill an oath he made to Abraham. The essence of His character—His holiness, His righteousness, His justice, His power—hangs on the fulfillment of that covenant. Because He has sworn with an oath that the Abrahamic covenant will be fulfilled, anything less means that He is extraordinarily unreliable.

You cannot put that covenant, or the God who made it, in the box of ancient history. The God of history is meeting you as I AM, inviting you to join Him as He accomplishes His purpose, even as He did that day with Moses. The story of His mission is actually the story of the Bible itself. His mission has played out over thousands of years, among millions of peoples, involving countless kings and kingdoms. He is headed to a definite conclusion with clearly explained outcomes.

As you meditate on the way God has connected your life to His, connect it to the remarkable record of moments when God encountered men, women, nations, and peoples throughout the Bible. He still encounters people today, and He wants to encounter you to join Him on His mission to the world.

Reality #5: God's invitation for you to work with Him always leads you to a crisis of belief that requires faith and action. Moses asked God, "Who am I, that I should go to Pharaoh and bring the Israelites out of Egypt?" (Exod. 3:11). That's not the question! In effect, God said to Moses, "It is not who you are but who I am! You're considering your identity instead of My identity. It's My identity that's going to make the difference in the exodus." God reveals His identity in the promise of His presence. He said, "I will be with you. And this will be the sign to you that it is I who have sent you: When you have brought the people out of Egypt, you will worship God on this mountain" (v. 12).

God leads us today by applying His Word to very specific situations. That happened to Moses here. God said, "It's on this very mountain where you are standing, with the burning bush, that I will reveal Myself to the children of Israel." The possibility of God's revealing His presence to all His people on the mountain where he stood must have encouraged Moses. Without that promise, Moses might never have done what he did. He could have quit many times, except for God's promise that this was going to happen.

God revealed to Moses a new name—I AM WHO I AM (Exod. 3:14). The bush wasn't just about the God of history but about the glory of His presence in all ages. God made a new, deeper revelation about His purposes as He declared to Moses who He is. He revealed to Moses a new dimension of His name, a personal name to go beside the historical one. The God of that historical, purpose-driven covenant is also present tense: I AM.

From mere curiosity in turning aside to see the burning bush, Moses' faith in Jehovah developed steadily from crisis to crisis. God reveals Himself to you to increase your faith as He did with Moses. Then God reveals His purposes to you so that you will do His will. Once you know who He is and what He wants to do, He desires that you seek to do His will in order to accomplish His purpose for His glory.

You, like Moses, may be facing a crisis of faith through which God has, is, or will speak to you. Look at the crises of faith in your life from all angles to see what God is really doing in your life through them.

Reality #6: You must make major adjustments in your life to join God in what He is doing. The miracle of God's connection with your life is that He does not just come one time and then disappear back into heaven. When you read, meditate on Scripture, pray, and join your life with other believers, God continues to encounter you and require adjustments in your life to join what He is doing.

If you see the purpose of God—His overarching plan to redeem humankind and regain His kingdom—as a mighty, rushing river headed to the very throne, you realize that standing against that force will either knock you down or cause you to be washed up on the shore. To be in line with the purpose of God, align your life with the direction of that mighty river of His will.

How many signals of what He's about to do does God have to give you to make you curious enough to follow? How does God speak to you? I look back on my life and wonder how many times I have missed what God intended for me. I'm thankful for the times I did listen. Sometimes we feel that God works only occasionally in our lives, but really He's working all the time. It's not just when a bush burns that God speaks. Be alert for God's voice.

God uses many ways to capture your attention. I've learned to pay attention to God when I'm discontented, for often He is getting ready to speak to me. When something that I don't understand stirs in me, that's God trying to get me ready to listen to Him. Many times I haven't been willing to listen until this growing discontentment reaches a crescendo.

The experience with God at the burning bush caught Moses' attention. But don't get so caught up in the encounter with God that you forget the point of the experience. You may think your version of a "burning bush" is the end-all and be-all of your faith. An encounter with God will always require action on your part.

Did Moses remember that early burning-bush experience? It was etched on his memory forever. Will you remember your burning bush? Only if you recognize God speaking to you through it. Be assured, however, that He is speaking, inviting, working to accomplish His purpose. If you listen with the perspective that He is indeed accomplishing His mission, you will find new ways to pray and new ways to minister in the situations that you face. For every event that pops up before you or slams full force into you, remember that the God of the universe is at work.

It is quite possible through reading this book you will discover that God wants you to make a major adjustment in your life. Don't run from it. Don't stick your head in the sand and ignore it. Face the matter squarely. Ask first and always, "Is this of God?"

Reality #7: You come to know God by experience as you obey Him and He accomplishes His purpose through you. Experiences with God are not just random encounters where God happens to drop into the stream of life to pluck someone from some upcoming, personal peril. Rather, the Bible shows you an unmistakable purpose, an unswerving plan that permeates every encounter between God and people. When He meets you, He is always headed in the same direction, citing the same theme, claiming the same final outcome that all peoples of the earth glorify Him!

Through Moses God revealed Himself as I AM WHO I AM whose plan is to show His glory through His people who are to be a kingdom of priests to all peoples. That was a remarkable revelation to Moses, and it may be to you!

If you were to tell me your story, you could probably relate a series of encounters you have had with God. Reflect on your experiences with God. Think about a time when you most vividly, most directly, remember experiencing God in your life. God is doing something specific and definable in your life. That something has not changed from the days of Abraham. It is something that will end only at the throne when people from every nation, tribe, and tongue join in one loud and persistent chorus of praise. That something is connecting your life to His purposes!

MOSES' WIDE-ANGLE LIFETIME EXPERIENCE WITH THE SPIRITUAL MARKERS

As dramatic as Moses' experience with God was at the burning bush, God had planned many more experiences with Moses during his lifetime. At this point we need to step back from that thrilling initial experience to see all God was going to do through

Moses' entire life. Don't stop with a single experience with God. Experience Him all your life!

Spiritual Marker #1: God chooses you to be on mission with Him to reconcile a lost world to Himself. When God chose Moses, He knew all of Moses' weaknesses, even though Moses insisted on reminding God about them. The Lord answered every excuse. God knew that He would work mightily in Moses' life to move him from weakness to strength throughout his lifetime because He had chosen him (Exod. 3:11–4:17).

Even in the terrible and seemingly hopeless situations now occurring in the world, God has chosen someone to intercede. As bad as the matter may be, He has not left it dangling in the wind. How can you be sure? For one thing God has put it on the hearts of His people and perhaps your heart. The things He brings before you can help you see where He is at work. Are you praying for God to work in a specific situation in the world now? God is absolutely determined to regain His kingdom! Here's His strategy that He revealed to Moses: He has chosen to use a holy priesthood, a chosen people, who will represent Him to the nations and bring the people of those nations before His throne to worship Him throughout eternity.

Spiritual Marker #2: God calls you to Himself to be on mission with Him. Just as you cannot escape His kingdom's inevitability, you also cannot escape His kingdom's call. To be allowed to behold His glory, to benefit from His blessing, to participate in His goodness calls for a commitment to His purpose. He cannot—will not—show His power in your life only to have you sully His reputation with contempt or indifference or fear or complaints.

71

God does not seek leaders when He calls people, because He is the Leader. He seeks servants who will let Him lead. Moses said, "I'm not worthy, Lord, to do this." God says, "I know. That's why I'm calling you to follow Me." The Scriptures say Moses was the meekest man in all the earth—a servant. Having abilities to lead is not important, but knowing who the leader is and letting Him lead is vital. Psalm 103:7 says, "He made known his ways to Moses, his deeds to the people of Israel." Anyone can see God's works, but God showed Moses His ways. God wants an intimate relationship with you so that you will know where He's going next by knowing His ways. Let's learn from Moses how to experience God's ways with individuals.

Way of God #1: He takes ordinary things and people and does extraordinary things with them. God told Moses to throw his staff on the ground. Moses obeyed, and it turned into a snake (Exod. 4:1–11). He told him to pick it up, and it turned back into his staff. "'This,' said the LORD, 'is so that they may believe that the LORD, the God of their fathers—the God of Abraham, the God of Isaac and the God of Jacob—has appeared to you'" (v. 5). God was saying, "I'm going to show my wonders to people through you, an ordinary person with an ordinary staff, so they will know who I am and glorify Me!"

God took the only thing Moses had—his staff—and parted the waters of the Red Sea, led the children of Israel out of Egypt, and brought forth water from the rock. Give back to God whatever He has given you, and He will use it in His kingdom in extraordinary ways for His glory!

Way of God #2: He expects you to obey His instructions whether they make sense or not. Can you imagine how Moses felt when God said, "Pick the snake up by the tail." You never pick up a snake by the tail because it will bite you. After forty years in the desert, Moses could have lectured God on how not to pick up snakes! When God tells you to do something, He expects you to do it whether it makes sense or not.

Way of God #3: When you obey, things won't always turn out as you thought they would. God said, "Put your hand in your cloak." When Moses pulled the hand out, "it was leprous" (v. 6). God expects your obedience even when things don't turn out as you expected. It isn't a mistake; He's building your faith. If you understood it, it wouldn't be faith. God uses your obedience to move you into what He is doing.

When you obey and things get worse, start praising God, because He is about to reveal something or do something far beyond what you can imagine! You may be right at the center of God's will when things get worse. God said to Moses, "Put your hand back in your cloak." Moses might have said, "If I put my hand in the first time and got leprosy, what will I get the next time?" But when Moses obeyed and put his hand in his cloak, it came out restored (v. 7).

Way of God #4: God tells you just enough for you to know what to do next. Moses had another concern: "What if they don't believe these signs?" God said, "Well, beyond these signs I have just shown you, you will take water out of the Nile and turn it to blood" (Exod. 4:8–9).

God showed Moses only three signs, but he was going to need ten plagues! God usually doesn't tell you all that will happen. He gives you just enough to walk by faith. That way He can lead you step by step, day by day, to do exactly what He wants you to do. He tells you only what you need to know. Then He says, "I will give you the ability to do whatever I ask, even though you've never been there before."

Moses insisted on holding on to one fear in particular—he could not speak plainly. This unwillingness to trust God to do whatever was required to mold Moses into a man that God could use would cause Moses a great deal of grief.

God finally sent Aaron to be the mouth for Moses, but the price was high. It was Aaron who made the golden calf. God desired to use Moses directly, but Moses wouldn't agree to that. This scenario should, at the very least, make us hesitant to make excuses to God! In His grace, He has decided He will use ordinary people through whom He will do extraordinary things—so He will get the glory from it. God is developing an obedient people so He will get the glory!

Today God moves in unprecedented ways. A precedent may not exist for what God calls you to do. Moses was disturbed by God's call. You also may struggle with it. What will the Lord have to do to get your attention?

When God calls you, respond. If you don't, God will respond in one or more ways. He may call you more emphatically, even troubling your mind daily. He may move other believers to support the call and remind you of it. He may discipline you to bring you back in line with His purpose. Or He may withdraw the call after a time and remove the possible blessing you would have received from it.

Spiritual Marker #3: God initiates a covenant of promise and obedience with you. God looked on His people and wanted to end their slavery because the Hebrew people's prayers caused Him to remember His covenant with them (Exod. 3:6–12). Could it have been they were praying about this very covenant? Praying not just, "Please help us get free. Please stop our suffering. Please do something." But rather, "God, You have a promise to fulfill. God, we have a mission to complete in the promised land. Help us fulfill our destiny!"

God affirmed the eternal significance of the covenant with Abraham. In Psalm 105:8–10, words like "forever," "for a thousand generations," and "everlasting" certainly show that God took a long view of that promise to Abraham. The psalmist speaks of "the oath he swore," or God's "decree," or the "covenant" itself. This helps you to focus on the fact that the driving purpose of the exodus was God's covenant and His determination to see it fulfilled. The purpose behind all of the glorious acts listed in Psalm 105 is His covenant with Abraham and its reaffirmation to Moses. The key to understanding the Bible and what God is doing in this age is to understand His mission: People are free to do as they will, but God works in all situations to lead people to His ultimate purpose to be acknowledged as Lord of all!

Why the deliverance of the Hebrews? What is the reason for this story? It was that the name of the Lord be proclaimed in all the earth. The God who wanted the world to know Him and glorify Him orchestrated this exodus! Egypt's position of being one of the world's leading nations guaranteed that the other nations would hear of a God that could deliver 1.5 million slaves from its bondage (Exod. 9:13–17).

A missionary in Central Asia thanked God for Marx and Stalin in the presence of International Mission Board President Jerry Rankin. Jerry asked how the missionary could pray such a prayer. The missionary answered, "I praise God that the Soviet Union has dominated these people groups for seventy years! This area was the stronghold that has been propagating the Islamic faith for generations, but in a mere seventy years of Communist domination with its atheistic ideology that stronghold has been emasculated, leaving the people spiritually destitute and open to the gospel." A worldwide movement of prayer for freedom in Russia was launched two years before the fall of Communism. God honored His covenant with His praying people. Although millions died in the purges of China's Mao Tse Tung, his regime wiped out ancestor worship and many of the family ties that kept many Chinese from Christ. Since the Communists came to power in China in 1949, the Christian population has grown from 750,000 to a reported 75–100 million!

Spiritual Marker #4: God prepares you for His mission. Because of His promise to Abraham, God began to seriously prepare Moses for his task at the burning bush by revealing His nature. If he didn't know it before, that day Moses learned that God's holiness demanded his respect. The unquenched fire in the bush—the real eternal flame—showed him that God is eternal. His statement, "I am the God of your father, the God of Abraham, the God of Isaac, the God of Jacob," demonstrated that God is personal. God showed His concern for His people who cried out to Him in their bondage. God demonstrated His faithfulness by telling them He would give them the promised land. God continues to reveal Himself to you today just as He did to Moses. He is the I AM who is the present, past, and future in a way we cannot understand. He reveals Himself to you—not only as holy God, a personal God, and a historical God but also as everlasting God. "I AM."

Once, as I landed in Cyprus, I began to wonder how God looks at Cyprus. I remembered that Cyprus was the first place missionaries went when the Holy Spirit sent Paul and Barnabas on their first missions trip. It was the first place that a leader of government accepted Christ as Savior. It was just south of that island that Paul went on his way to prison in Rome. I had just read the psalm that says, "A day is as a thousand years to the Lord, and a thousand years is as a day." The Lord said to me, "Avery, do you realize that from My perspective, it was just day before yesterday that Paul and Barnabas came here, and it was just two days before that that Moses led the children of Israel out of Egypt. And tomorrow is A.D. 3000." Wow! God showed me that He is the everlasting "I AM!"

Moses' ongoing preparation included repeated challenges from Pharaoh and the people of Israel. Even when he grew discouraged and complained to God—just as the Israelites complained to Him—the Lord patiently encouraged him and prepared His instrument to act on His behalf to fulfill His promise to free His people from slavery.

Spiritual Marker #5: God sends you to the place where He can best work through you to accomplish His mission. God said, "And now the cry of the Israelites has reached me, and I have seen the way the Egyptians are oppressing them. So now, go. I am sending you to Pharaoh to bring my people the Israelites out of Egypt" (Exod. 3:9–10). Moses could not stay on the backside of the desert and still go with God. God moved him to the place He could best use him. God sent Moses to Egypt so He could move His people to the promised land.

How God worked in Moses' life can also apply to how God works in your own life. After studying why God raised up Moses, what do you think God has raised you up to do for Him? What do you think He wants to show you? What is it that He wants you to proclaim? Keep asking those questions as you read.

Spiritual Marker #6: God guides you on His mission. In dealing with Pharaoh, the most powerful ruler on the face of the earth, Moses needed God's careful guidance at every step on His mission. Moses and Aaron were faithful in speaking God's words to this great king of Egypt.

The Lord knew Pharaoh would harden his heart, so He prepared Moses for the response. Because the proud ruler of Egypt reacted this way, God hardened his heart further until he and his whole army were totally destroyed. God told Moses what to say and informed him of the outcome ahead of time. Nine times God told Moses that he would speak to Pharaoh with no success!

Why did God send Moses ten times to Pharaoh? Each plague was God's testimony of power against a specific Egyptian deity. Egyptian home and tomb decorations depict Ra (the sun god), bulls, scarabs, water of the Nile, frogs, and others. By the time the plagues were finished, Pharaoh and the Egyptians had seen Jehovah confound the power of every deity they worshiped. It should also have made a lasting impression on Israel. They should have been convinced forever that their God was the only One to be worshiped.

Nevertheless, our hero hit bottom several times. He wanted to give up as these five major difficulties ensued:

- Pharaoh reacted by making the task harder after each plague.
- The Israelites faced the Red Sea when Pharaoh pinned them in between the mountains, the sea, the desert, and his army.

- After their victory when they needed water, the Israelites wanted to lynch Moses and return to Egypt.
- Israel worshiped a golden calf, breaking the first two commandments.
- The people refused to trust God enough to take the promised land.

Unfortunately, throughout their wilderness wanderings, the Israelites mirrored Moses' initial weakness of not trusting God. As a result of their lack of faith and obedience, the whole generation of which Moses was a part (including its leader) was not permitted to enter the promised land. Under such trying circumstances, I think I would have complained and become as angry as Moses did. How would you have fared as leader of 1.5 million people upon whom God had passed judgment and told them that all those over twenty years of age would die before the people went into the promised land?

Because they were His children, God had both the right and the obligation to discipline Israel. This discipline involved nurture for motivation, training for obedience, and punishment for correction in righteousness. How often God expressed anguish at His people's refusal to become His holy possession and fulfill His will! But He punished them each time. The Lord repeatedly sent tests and tragedies to curb the prideful spirit of His people. Only Joshua and Caleb followed God wholeheartedly and were rewarded accordingly. Sadly, it took a whole new generation that had not seen the Red Sea deliverance to obey God and to conquer the land He had promised to His people.

Spiritual Marker #7: God uses you to bring glory to His name through His mission. The ancient world was crisscrossed by caravans of merchants, traders, ambassadors of nations, and any person from Africa, India, or China who wanted an excuse to visit this area of wealth and wonder. Encamped on the trip back home, these people told of the Egyptian events, attributing them all to Israel's God, Jehovah. God's deeds became known everywhere.

The final act of God's deliverance of Israel from bondage was about to be played out on Egypt's stage. As every Egyptian home echoed with weeping and wailing when the firstborn were found dead—fathers, sons, husbands, brothers, even the male animals— the Israelites must have been awed that God had spared them by directing the death angel to pass over them. In fleeing from Pharaoh's regime, they plundered the Egyptians of articles of silver and gold and clothing as the Lord gave them favor with their former taskmasters.

Amid the mourning, Pharaoh suddenly realized what he had done; every one of the slaves was gone! Meanwhile the Israelites, led as God displayed His glory in a pillar of cloud by day and a pillar of fire by night, moved hastily to encamp where God directed on the Red Sea shores. The showdown between God and Egypt was underway!

The Egyptians did not understand; the great I AM was in control. Pharaoh's chariots reached the middle of the Red Sea as the last of the Hebrews stepped out on the opposite bank. God rolled back the piled-up waters, drowning Pharaoh's horses and charioteers. God intervened in the history of one of the world's greatest nations, proving Himself greater than any king or kingdom (Exod. 14:4, 18, 31).

MOSES' 180-DEGREE CORPORATE EXPERIENCE WITH GOD'S PEOPLE AND THE SPIRITUAL MARKERS

God never works with just one individual when He is on mission. Not Moses. Not you. He uses individuals to influence His people to be on mission with Him. Moses was God's instrument to awaken His people and to equip them.

God reveals Himself by His acts. The creation, the flood, and the confusion of tongues at Babel helped early people know that God was powerful and involved with their daily lives. The Egyptians learned God's power by His triumph over their gods. After the exodus, the Israelites certainly noticed their chosen status as a treasured nation. The plagues and the parting of the Red Sea revealed that God was capable of changing the course of history on behalf of His people.

God set about to plant this treasured possession to be a showcase to the world. Israel was to serve as a kingdom of priests and a holy nation, thus connecting people back to Creator God. An attention grabber in the exodus drama is the way God revealed that He would go about gaining worldwide recognition. During the exodus itself, the nation of Israel first became conscious of their own role in God's unfolding plan.

Even in its privileged, spiritual position, Israel did not perceive God's ways. A difference exists in knowing God's acts and knowing God's ways (Ps. 103:7). Anyone can see God's deeds, like the Red Sea opening or water flowing from a rock, but only a few know His ways. After more than forty years of intimate relationships in marriage, I know my wife's ways, and she knows mine. Shirley and I have been separated in a foreign city and found each other by knowing how the other would think in a given situation.

81

Do you know the ways of God with His people? As Moses prepared to end his earthly journey, he told Israel the ways of God with His people in terms they could remember. I recommend that you read Exodus 19:4–6 and Deuteronomy 32:9–12 to discover God's ways and how He leads His people. God trains His people for their mission as eagles train their young to fly!

Way of God with His people #1: He stirs up their nest to get them on His agenda. When an eagle gets ready to build its nest, it finds a crag or a ledge where wild animals cannot get to it. There the eagle weaves such a large, solid nest out of sticks, branches, briars, or bones that even the high, swirling winds cannot blow it down. Then she lines that nest with feathers, cloth, papers, or anything soft for comfort. The eaglets hatch in that cozy environment. A baby eagle is safe. Above is a mother to protect from the rain with curb service at least three times a day!

The mother eagle knows that these eagles were not born to sit in a nest all of their lives. When the time arrives for them to fly, she reaches into the nest, pulls out all the soft down and paper with her claw, and lets the little eaglets down on the briars, sticks, bones, and branches. They begin to cry out because everywhere they turn they get stuck.

That is what God says He did to Israel; He stirred up their nest. God had given the Israelites the choicest part of Egypt in the land of Goshen when Joseph was the second in command in Egypt. For four hundred years Israel was nurtured in this nest. The people had forgotten much about the promised land except that Joseph requested that they take back his bones. God stirred up their nest. When you get stuck in one of the stages of development, one of God's ways is to make you uncomfortable by stirring your nest, readying you for His next move.

These free people, who had been assured a promised land in which to live, found themselves building storehouses for pagan Pharaoh. That was not what they were meant to be! God had to get them where He wanted them to go, so He let them fall into the hands of a Pharaoh who enslaved them and made their lives miserable. They began to cry out to the Lord. God works with His people this way: He stirs their nest in such a way that they cry out to the Lord. When Israel cried out, God called Moses and said, "I have heard the cries of my people, and I am going to save them." God must get us where we are ready to cry out to Him and say, "God, do something. Somehow, we are not all You promised we would be. We are not doing all we are supposed to be doing."

When I was pastor of Inglewood Baptist Church in Grand Prairie, Texas, a Dallas suburb, God began to stir our nest. I sensed He wanted to bring revival, but the normal means had brought only ordinary results. I challenged the church by saying, "As I have studied revivals of God's people in the Bible and history, they did not just set a date, schedule a preacher, and do the ordinary things we do to promote revival. They prayed until God sent revival, and then they asked a neighboring pastor or whomever God appointed to preach." That suburban church voted to follow this historic model. I encouraged members to do whatever God told them to do—have prayer meetings in their homes, make a poster, or whatever.

Four months passed; revival had not occurred. I took four men with me to an evangelism conference. Revival for us did not start with the great preaching but with the testimony in the halls when a pastor friend of mine and four laymen testified of a sweeping revival in their church and in their city. God used that experience

83

to call us to pray every night until God sent revival. He revealed our sins, and we began to confess them. On Layman's Day this confession spread to the entire congregation. I said, "Obviously, God has sent revival. Whom should we ask to preach beginning tomorrow night?" The men of the church volunteered, and fifteen of them preached for the next two weeks. God changed the church. Two of the men and I went to Japan on a mission trip and saw six hundred professions of faith in three weeks. Today, eight couples from that church serve as missionaries. God stirred our nest to teach us to fly by faith.

God may be stirring your nest to help you and your church wake up to His mission. He may be asking you to take a step of faith. If you don't respond to Him, you will be miserable and make those around you miserable. God is stirring His people all over the world to join Him on mission. As I write this, I have concluded trips to every part of the world to meet with leaders of Great Commission Christian organizations and leaders of Baptist conventions. God is stirring them in unprecedented ways to join Him in taking the gospel to every people group in the world and to establish churches among them. Is God stirring your nest so your church will join Him on mission? (Heb. 12:5–13).

Way of God with His people #2: He demonstrates His power by hovering over His people. After the eagle stirs the nest, she hovers over the nest with her wings to show the eaglets how big she is. In effect, she says, "Never fear; mother is here. I know you are sitting on briars. I know you are still crying, but don't worry. I have everything under control." While Israel was stirred up, God sent ten plagues to show how mighty and powerful He really is! God was hovering over Israel so the Israelites would trust Him and leave their nest to go to the promised land.

When the eagle hovers over the nest, the eaglets realize how big their mother is. Her wingspan can be from five to twelve feet. She hovers to free them from worry. After God stirs your nest, He hovers over you. He shows you He is everything you need. God wants you to understand He is big enough to accomplish His mission. When He stirs your nest, God then hovers over you, not to make you comfortable but to cause you to believe Him for the next thing He wants to do in your life. How has God been showing you Himself and His power to your church?

Way of God with His people #3: God leads His people to take the next step on mission with Him by bearing them on His wings and then shaking them off. The next thing the mother eagle does is to place her wing on the edge of the nest and say to the eaglets, "Get off the briars and get on the wing." If they won't do it, she starts beating them until they do. It seems that even their mother has turned against them! God's way is to stir you up, hover over you with His wings, and then bear you up on His wings. Sometimes God has to let you get beaten up by circumstances until you say, "I'll take anything but this." At that point you get on the wing.

Once the eaglets get on her wing, the mother lurches off the cliff and begins to fly. For the first time in their lives, they experience the ecstasy of flight. As they soar through the air, they begin to understand what they were born to do. The mother eagle takes them back to the nest. They jump back into the briars and jump right back on her wing. Again she takes them high above the earth. This time, while they are enjoying their flight, she shakes them off. They go tumbling down. Some fly, and some don't. She dives under those that can't fly and catches them. Again she takes them up to the heights, lets them relax, and shakes them off again until they learn how to fly. Another method she sometimes uses is to take them to the edge of the cliff and just push them over. God puts His people in a faith-creating situation to get them to fly in order to fulfill the purpose for which He created them.

God bore Israel on eagles' wings and again and again demonstrated that He was sufficient when the Hebrews flew by faith. In all kinds of ways—the miracles in Egypt, at the Red Sea, the manna, the quail, and the water out of the rock—He showed that He wanted them to step out in faith. If they fell, He picked them up and took them up again and again to teach them to fly. As you reflect on what happened to Israel, recall a circumstance in which you felt God "pushed you or your church off the cliff" or when God "shook you into the air to cause you to fly by faith."

At the beginning of God's covenant with Israel, He promised the people they would be a holy nation and a kingdom of priests, reflecting His glory. At the close of the age, God has decreed that His people will be called "priests of the Lord" and "ministers of our God" (2 Pet. 2:9–11; Rev. 1:6). God never wavers in His purpose. He chose the tribe of Levi to be priests and models of what the nation was to become. Old Testament priests brought Israel before God to worship and experience the glory of His holiness. Although the priests had many duties, they had two key functions: (1) representing God to people and (2) representing people to God. God intended Israel to perform these two functions in relation to the nations.

If the entire nation were to function as priests, to whom were they to be priests? Not only to themselves but also to the nations. God's intention was clear. But Israel misunderstood, misinterpreted, or rejected it. At this stage God did not intend for the

Israelites to take the initiative in converting the nations to God but to be faithful and to become His people so they could reflect His glory. At the right time, Israel was to proclaim salvation to the whole world. Unfortunately, Israel rebelled, never living up to its missionary potential.

The Lord of heaven and earth expects His people today to be priestly people and suffering people, willing to lay down our lives to serve others. We are to be an obedient, holy, disciplined, and missionary people. We are to love, serve, suffer, and minister as God does to all people. We are to take the salvation message to the entire world.

As with Israel, God brings His people today to a decision point. He brings you to the place where you must exercise faith—stepping out on a limb that you don't know will hold you up. When you step out in faith, you find God has provided wings—the wings of faith. You begin to fly and fulfill the purpose for which God has designed you! It's glorious! God's people may be at such a point. We will either believe God and follow Him, or history will record the story of our bleached bones in the desert.

THE 360-DEGREE ETERNAL PERSPECTIVE

What are the eternal truths that God revealed to us through Moses? Here are three of them.

Eternal Revelation #1: God is on mission so that the knowledge of His glory will cover the earth as the waters do the sea! You cannot fully understand God's mission without understanding why He insists that all the earth acknowledge Him as Lord. He expects you to give Him the glory due Him because He is

God—to bow before Him as Lord above all and to serve Him (Exod. 33:15–19).

Here you come face to face with God's purpose-driven mission to reclaim His kingdom and in that process to redeem humanity. But make no mistake about it: what He does, He does for His name's sake—not just for our salvation or for our good only. Yes, He reigns and redeems with love, and we certainly gain both salvation and incredible good from His reign. But reign He does, and He expects our worship, our adoration, and our praise because He alone is God. His own glory is at the epicenter of all that He does!

Moses' victory song after the victory at the Red Sea (Exod. 15, and especially verse 11) captures Israel's awe and adoration of our incredible God, who reigns supreme over all that is, was, and ever will be.

"Who among the gods is like you, O LORD? Who is like you— majestic in holiness, awesome in glory, working wonders?" God is majestic in holiness. God's holiness manifests at least three things; He is the standard of holiness; He is Other (meaning different in kind); and He is love.

God is so majestic that He towers above all gods and religions, philosophies, cultures, and all people, including the greatest kings, presidents, and generals. His holiness is the standard for truth, righteousness, and faithfulness. He is different from His creation, humans, and all other gods. He shows His majestic love by His mercy in forgiving us our sins and giving us eternal life.

- *God is awesome in glory.* Everyone who has come into God's presence has been overwhelmed (Exod. 33:18–21; 34:5–7). Moses only saw the backside of God, but he saw more than anybody else ever had! When Ezekiel saw

God's glory, he was overwhelmed with God. Isaiah said, "Woe to me! . . . I am ruined. For I am a man of unclean lips, and I live among a people of unclean lips" (Isa. 6:5). Job said at the end of his complaining, dialogue, and debate, "I know that you can do all things; no plan of yours can be thwarted. . . . Surely I spoke of things I did not understand, things too wonderful for me to know" (Job 42:2–3). The glory of the things of this world—athletic success, space exploration, the beauty of nature, or anything else you can think of—in no way compares to the glory of God. God is awesome in glory!

- *God is all-powerful.* I once heard the great pastor R. G. Lee describe the magnitude of space and then contrast that to the intricacies of the smallest of the atoms in your little finger. He said that you have whole space systems in miniature in one end of your little finger. It is amazing what God has put together. The Bible is the story of God making His glory known to His people and His people reflecting that glory to the peoples of the world (Ps. 96).

Eternal Revelation #2: God's glory is His presence among His people. When the Israelites made a golden calf to worship, God told Moses He would not go with them into the promised land. Moses interceded, asking Him not to send them to the promised land unless His presence went before them. Moses did not want Israel to enter the promised land unless God's presence went along (Exod. 33:12–18). He had three reasons for this:

1. God's presence would show that they were God's people.
2. God's presence would demonstrate God's favor—that He was pleased with them.
3. The glory of God's presence would distinguish them from all other peoples.

Although the passage mentions all three, the most significant to Moses was that God's presence would distinguish Israel from other peoples. Today the distinguishing mark of our lives and of our churches should be the presence of God.

Eternal Revelation #3: God's glory involves our going on mission with Him. Once you understand that God's purpose to see His glory proclaimed among the nations is the mission that drives His every encounter with you, you begin to see what an incredible blessing it is to participate in God's mission. To join God on His mission is to be assured that your life will be eternally successful!

Every year Shirley and I host in our home about a thousand new missionaries who have answered God's call to serve overseas. Repeatedly I hear stories of people who give up successful careers and lifestyles in America to answer God's call. To the uninformed their actions may seem foolish, but they, like Moses, see the eternal blessings yet to come from proclaiming God's glory to others. His presence distinguishes us from all the peoples who don't know God through Christ.

As we conclude our study of Moses, let me ask you some important questions. What is it God wants more than anything else? What does God want His people to be? I'm surprised how many people are confounded by those questions because they should be so obvious and so simple. God wants all people to wor-

ship and glorify Him. He expects His people to be a holy kingdom of priests to bring all peoples to Him. Moses understood
God's desire. Do you?

4

DAVID ON MISSION WITH GOD

ESTABLISHING A KINGDOM
WITHOUT END

Ascribe to the LORD, O families of nations,
ascribe to the LORD glory and strength, ascribe to the
Lord the glory due his name. Bring an offering and
come before him; worship the LORD in the splendor of
his holiness.

—1 Chronicles 16:28–29

LISTENING TO NIGERIAN PRESIDENT OLUSEGUN OBASANJO SPEAK during the 150th anniversary celebration of Baptist work in his country, I could hardly believe how God had raised up this man from anonymity and imprisonment to be president of the largest country in Africa. As a boy, Obasanjo experienced Jesus Christ as Lord and Savior while a student at Abeokuta Baptist Boys High School in his hometown. His father, once a successful farmer, had

93

suffered financial hardships and left the family just before his son began high school. After graduation the younger Obasanjo worked in a clerical position and then taught religion and science at the African Church Modern School. Though he wished to attend college, he could not afford it, so he joined the army.

He moved up in the army's ranks until, as commander of Third Marine Commando Division, he accepted the Biafran surrender ending the Nigerian Civil War in 1970. In 1975, General Murtala Muhammed and Obasanjo led a bloodless coup, after which Muhammed became head of state and named Obasanjo chief of staff of the Nigerian army. In 1976, Muhammed was assassinated, and Obasanjo assumed leadership of Nigeria, becoming the first Yoruba president. While in office, Obasanjo challenged British colonialism in Africa and adopted a new constitution in 1978 that guaranteed some basic human rights. He held free elections in 1979, as he promised, but lost narrowly. He became the only military ruler in the nation's history to voluntarily step down. He then started a farming company, raising chickens and pigs and growing bananas.

In 1993, General Sani Abacha became head of state in yet another coup and accused Abiola, who apparently had won the presidency in an election, and Obasanjo of treason and plotting a coup. They were both jailed for life, together with about forty others, some of whom received death sentences for charges that were never revealed. After an international outcry, Abacha reduced the sentence, but Obasanjo spent three years in prison. After Abacha's sudden death, elections were held. This time Obasanjo won the presidency by a 62 percent vote.

During an interview with him at the dedication of the first Protestant chapel on the presidential grounds, I presented him a Nigerian copy of *Experiencing God* and the *Experiencing God Study Bible*. I said, "Your story parallels a lot the story of King David, who went through ten difficult years before he finally became king." He replied, "I love David, and I wrote a book in prison that I call *The Youth of God*. David is one of my 'miracle children.'" The president told about how he had begun to study *MasterLife* in prison and then had been moved to another prison, where he recommitted his life to Christ and wrote four Christian books. He moved from being a nobody to a somebody that God could use in His body.

Do you ever feel like you are a nobody in God's eyes? You compare yourself to others—perhaps to your fellow church members or other Christians you know—and feel as if you come up short. You think, *I don't have any special abilities. I've never served in any important role. I'm just an ordinary person. How can God use me?*

Most important biblical figures started out on their walk with God in much the same way. David was a "little person"—the underdog—in one of the greatest dramas of the Bible.

DAVID'S CLOSE-UP VIEW OF THE SEVEN REALITIES OF EXPERIENCING GOD

God revealed Himself step by step to David, and David responded so positively that God accomplished mighty things through Him. From giant-killer to sweet psalmist of Israel, David was a remarkably skilled servant of God who reveled in God's glory.

David's encounter with Goliath set the pace for David's experiences with God. However, the truly mighty thing that David did in his encounter with Goliath was much more significant than simply toppling a wicked giant. God's purpose for David, the little person in this famous skirmish, involved all the peoples of the world (1 Sam. 17:45–47).

God's purpose locally was to show the Philistines and Israelites that the battle was the Lord's and that He would win it. His purpose globally was that by telling the story, the whole world would know God and His glory. God was making Himself a name through David.

Reality #1: God is always at work around you demonstrating the glory of His presence. In Psalm 139:1–6, David acknowledges that God was involved in everything he did, said, or thought. He experienced God's glory in every aspect of life. David's words can be your words, too. Do you identify with David's words in Psalm 139?

We first meet David when Samuel is told to anoint one of the sons of Jesse whom God had chosen to become Saul's successor (1 Sam. 16:1). People often overlooked David because he was the youngest and was a shepherd. Often the one God uses is the one others overlook. God told Samuel, when he thought the first son, Eliab, was to be anointed, "Do not consider his appearance or his height, for I have rejected him. The LORD does not look at the things man looks at. Man looks at the outward appearance, but the LORD looks at the heart" (1 Sam. 16:7).

Finally, David was called in to meet Samuel, who saw that he was also "ruddy, with a fine appearance and handsome features"

(v. 12). Still Samuel realized that he could not depend on outward looks. "Then the LORD said, 'Rise and anoint him; he is the one.'"

Reality #2: God pursues a continuing love relationship with you that is both real and personal. God had special plans for David even before he was born in Bethlehem. In Psalm 22:9–10, David reflected on his knowledge of this. David was born into a nation of people experiencing God's judgment for desiring to have a king like their neighbors instead of having the Lord reign over them. God permitted them to have Saul, who started out well but was of a character totally different from David's. To replace Saul, God looked for someone whose heart would be turned toward Him. He found that quality in a little nobody who had a mundane job—shepherding—that slaves or females usually did. But David's time spent outdoors with the sheep gave him opportunity to talk to God and to listen to Him. David's psalms show that he experienced God's glory through a long-term intimate relationship with God.

You may believe that you are a nobody and that your daily life is made up of ordinary activities. If asked to list the activities of your days, you might list only such things as washing dishes, buying gasoline, buying groceries, earning a living, and caring for children. You may even think all your mundane tasks do not relate to God's mission. Look again! God has had His eye on you since before you were born. He has particular plans for you. God is always at work around you, and He is initiating an experience in which His glory is revealed in His real and personal love relationship with you.

Reality #3: God invites you to become involved with Him in His work. We have no details of how David responded to this invitation of God except for his expressions of humility and praise in his psalms. However, "from that day on the Spirit of the LORD came upon David in power" (v. 13). One of Saul's servants described David to the king like this, "I have seen a son of Jesse of Bethlehem who knows how to play the harp. He is a brave man and a warrior. He speaks well and is a fine-looking man. And the LORD is with him" (v. 18).

Later, when David took supplies to his brothers on the battle-front, David heard Goliath and immediately asked about the giant who defied the armies of God. When David volunteered to fight him, Saul said to him, "You are not able to go out against this Philistine and fight him; you are only a boy, and he has been a fighting man from his youth" (1 Sam. 17:33). David's stirring response was, "The LORD who delivered me from the paw of the lion and the paw of the bear will deliver me from the hand of this Philistine" (v. 37). David responded positively to God's second invitation to join Him on His mission. David understood the circumstances and what was at stake for God's name, which he revered. He knew that God wanted to show His glory so that "the whole world will know that there is a God in Israel" (v. 46b).

The David and Goliath story is about more than a young boy defeating a giant. God was fulfilling His mission through David. Today this story of David's defeating the giant is still being told all over the world to the delight of the thousands of people groups that are just being introduced to it.

Are your eyes open to ways God is inviting you to join Him? For instance, is a friend asking you questions about God? Or do you have an interest in people of other nationalities? Or do you have a deep hunger for the Word? Or are you considering giving to a specific Christian ministry? Be aware of how God is inviting you to join Him, even in ways you might be inclined to overlook.

Reality #4: God speaks to you by the Holy Spirit. The first detailed description of God's speaking to David appears when David challenged Goliath. Although he came to the front lines only to bring supplies to his brothers who mocked him, David's first response was, "Who is this uncircumcised Philistine that he should defy the armies of the living God?" (v. 26). The Spirit of God was working in David's heart to cause him to be jealous for God's name and God's covenant people. David did not see the giant as an invincible foe but as an opportunity for God to manifest His power.

We also know that David had heard the voice of God through the Scriptures because his statements to Goliath are previewed in Deuteronomy 20:1–19, where Moses told Israel how to fight against an enemy stronger than they. David knew God was with him, and that was all he needed.

Someone once said, "One plus God is a majority." But God is a majority all by Himself! Don't ask God to join you. You join Him, just as David did. David knew he was doing what the Lord wanted and that God was with him to bring glory to His name.

Think about how you see challenges you face. Do you see them as problems or as opportunities? Pray that God will show you by His Spirit how you are to join Him in His mission. Be aware of any confirmations you receive about this—in Scripture, prayer, circumstances, confirmation by the body, or the counsel of a trusted Christian.

Reality #5: God's invitation for you to work with Him always leads you to a crisis of belief that requires faith and action. If God has invited you to join Him, you have to make a decision. Either you will believe Him and act on it, or you will fail to obey and sit on it. David did not hesitate or dwell on his weaknesses. He spoke with confidence to Saul and Goliath. He acted on faith by refusing Saul's armor and instead picked up five smooth stones for his slingshot.

David's awareness of God's presence gave him faith. God had promised He would be with him as He had in the past. David could trust God. Some might call this naïveté or blind enthusiasm, but it was neither. It was faith in God who had called him and who had anointed him. He responded to Goliath's threats with, "This day the LORD will hand you over to me, and I'll strike you down and cut off your head. Today I will give the carcasses of the Philistine army to the birds of the air and the beasts of the earth, and the whole world will know that there is a God in Israel. All those gathered here will know that it is not by sword or spear that the LORD saves; for the battle is the LORD's, and he will give all of you into our hands" (1 Sam. 17:46–47).

Reality #6: You must make major adjustments in your life to join God in what He is doing. Perhaps David's major change began when Samuel anointed him. He went back to the fields to be a shepherd, but certainly he perceived the implications of the anointing. He must have wondered what he would become and what it could mean. He must have prayed much. His brothers' reaction indicates they saw him as different and envied him.

The obvious major adjustment occurred when David took supplies to his brothers on the battlefront. During that visit David went from being a shepherd, harpist, and delivery boy to being a soldier of the king. He went from being a nobody to being a national hero. Joining God on His mission changed his identity. Although it was a change in David and in his life, it was not a change in God's plan for him. All along God had planned that David would be on mission with Him and would fulfill a major part of God's revelation of Himself to the world!

By major adjustments, I am thinking about things such as changing jobs, rearranging your daily schedule, refusing to participate in a previous activity, spending more time in a regular devotional period, giving up something you love to do, and contacting a missions agency about some kind of service. What major adjustment is God asking you to make?

Reality #7: You experience God's glory as you obey Him and He accomplishes His purpose through you. David came to know God better as he experienced God's working through him that day to defeat Goliath! David saw Goliath's challenge of Israel and to God as a challenge to the name and power of Jehovah. David obeyed what he believed God had called him to do. Without obedience David would have missed God's plan for his life.

If we could only see what we have missed by our disobedience, we would cry out to God for one more opportunity to obey Him and to fulfill His mission in our lives. We cannot change the past, but we will be surprised by what God will accomplish through us if we obey Him. Even though David sometimes failed to obey, he showed deep repentance when he failed, and God still did much of what He had planned to do originally through him.

What has God asked you to do that you have not yet done? Delayed obedience is disobedience. Perhaps you have already delayed obeying what you know the Lord wants you to do. Do not despair. Delayed obedience is better than no obedience at all.

But don't delay any longer, lest you miss your intersection with God's purpose. Get on mission with Him!

When he killed Goliath, David was just beginning a lifetime of walking with God. He was seventy-one years old when he finished his course and went to be with the Lord forever. In the interim, God did tremendous things through David as he joined the Lord on mission.

DAVID'S WIDE-ANGLE LIFETIME EXPERIENCE OF FOLLOWING GOD'S SPIRITUAL MARKERS

Spiritual Marker #1: God chooses you to be on mission with Him. David alone of all the people in Israel was willing to face Goliath, because he knew he had been chosen for this moment in history, to do great exploits for God. The Lord was getting ready to exalt this God-honoring young man above everyone else and to turn the course of history for His nation, the children of Israel (Ps. 89:19–26).

Looking back at this event, you see the secret to David's success was the Lord's Spirit working mightily through him. God found him, anointed him, sustained him, and exalted him. God crushed his foes and struck down his enemies. God's faithful love did all of this for David, knowing that David would give God all the glory.

You are called on to fight many spiritual battles on your way through this world. The enemy will put many obstacles in your path, but the Lord wants you to become an overcomer as David was. When you rely on God and not yourself and when you are willing to give Him the glory, He will fight for you. Your hope during these crisis times is anchored in your confidence that God chose you for His purpose, and you know that He is faithful (Ps. 139:13–16).

Spiritual Marker #2: God calls you to Himself to be on mission with Him. The call of God comes in many disguises. David's call was dramatic and unexpected. On his way from the pasture, he must have wondered why his father had called him in the middle of the day. Samuel had already consecrated David's brothers, who stood to one side confused because Samuel had not chosen them. Jesse was proud that one of his sons was going to be chosen, but he was perplexed that Samuel passed over his first seven sons. Before David could grasp the significance of what was happening, Samuel poured oil all over him. Immediately David was aware that the Spirit of God was there (1 Sam. 16:13). Everyone knew that Samuel had anointed Saul as king in the same way. The significance of this act could not be missed. David evidently went back to tending the sheep. But the Spirit of the Lord began to speak to him and to help him understand what it meant to be chosen and called as the next king.

We tend to think that God's call has to occur in some dramatic experience like David's. But, as with Elijah, we know that God often speaks in a still, small voice. God speaks in a dramatic experience but also in a still, small voice or through the actions or words of others. Have you sensed God calling you, anointing you, or getting you ready for something? When you recognize that God has anointed you with the Holy Spirit, begin to ask Him what He has in mind.

This young man whom God had chosen to be king had many exploits ahead of him. For defeating Goliath, he became a hero in the people's eyes. Later, they sang, "Saul has slain his thousands, and David his tens of thousands." That could have gone to his head, but David was eager to give God the glory. After all, he was chosen to be on God's mission—not his own.

Spiritual Marker #3: God initiates a covenant of promise and obedience with you. The Lord made a covenant with David when Samuel anointed him to be king over Israel. Later David's experience with Jonathan gave him a living picture of what a covenant is. The first time Jonathan saw David, he "became one in spirit with David and he loved him as himself" (1 Sam. 18:1).

David learned afresh by his experience with Jonathan that God takes the initiative in His love and covenant. He realized that God loved him with a totally unselfish love. The gifts Jonathan gave David symbolized the kingdom that Jonathan should inherit but that God would give to David. David began to realize that "in everything he did he had great success, because the LORD was with him" (1 Sam. 18:14).

God made many promises to David, and David pledged his allegiance to God. However, God's covenant with David culminated when David wanted to build a house for God where the ark of the covenant could reside. Through the prophet Nathan, God told David he would not build the temple because he had shed blood. Then God turned the tables on David and promised to build him a house! God made at least nine promises to David in this covenant (2 Sam. 7:8–16).

David also committed himself to God and His glory. He gave God the glory for all his victories. He worshiped Him only. When the time came, he gave lavishly to build the temple and prepared the plans that God gave him so Solomon could build it.

In the Bible God makes more than three thousand promises to His people. Many He has made personally to you. His Holy Spirit communicates with you that the promises are for you. John 3:16 and Matthew 28:18–20 are two promises that all believers claim. Ask God to reveal promises that He has made in Scripture about your being on mission with Him.

God prepared David all his life. He chose him before his birth, called him from the sheep pasture, anointed him, and covenanted to bless him. God gave him physical abilities, knowledge, wisdom, emotional sensitivities, and spiritual perception and awareness. But it took time and experience to develop all of these characteristics in him.

Spiritual Marker #4: God prepares you for His mission. If you looked at David as a boy, you never would have guessed what God had in store for him. If you could compare your life with God's original plan, you would be elated by what He has planned and disappointed by what you have accomplished thus far. If you could step back and look at your whole life, you would be amazed at what God still is prepared to do through you!

David might have expected that he was ready to be king when Samuel anointed him. However, he would experience two more anointings before he ruled—first as king of Judah and then as king of all Israel. In between, he experienced ten grueling years while God prepared him for his assignment. When God calls you and makes a covenant to bless you, get ready for training, testing, and tribulation. This is what happened to David. He experienced Saul's jealous, murderous rages and attempts to kill him as well as many other hardships.

You, too, probably have experienced difficulties in your pilgrimage to follow God's leadership in your life. These difficulties may have included things such as the failure of your heroes, the jealousy of others, frequent moves and uprootings, life-threatening situations, and disapproval of family members. Whether you realize it or not, these have helped prepare you for your assignment. Be aware that God is at work in the midst of what seems like problems, shaping and forming you to become the person He intends for you to be.

From the time you are called until you fulfill that call lies a valley of testing. God must develop your character to match your assignment. When young preachers have a flush of success and receive accolades from their friends, they think they have arrived. God has just begun His work in them so He can work through them.

David developed many God-given skills. God prepared him as a brave warrior to fight Goliath, as a musician to write and to play the harp for Saul, as a leader to defeat the Philistines, and as a king to rule.

God prepares you by helping you develop your skills. God is using missionaries from hundreds of occupations. The twenty-first century could be called the Century of the Laity because secular skills allow laypeople to work and witness among people in restricted countries where traditional missionaries are not allowed. On the other hand, He teaches you that without Him you can do nothing. Sometimes He moves you in a direction opposite from your skills so you will depend totally on Him. Living in other countries I discovered God not only used skills I had developed but abilities I didn't know I had. Success depends not so much on your ability as on your availability and willingness to accept responsibility. As you join God on mission, He will show you the skills you need and equip you.

Spiritual Marker #5: God sends you to the place where He can best work through you to accomplish His purpose and bring glory to God. David couldn't remain a shepherd and be used of God as king. God had to get him out of his father's house to the king's palace and then to the battlefield in order to prepare him for his important role. What if he had said, "No, thanks. I'm comfortable here. I like being a shepherd. I like staying near my family. Find someone else who is restless and ambitious"? Then God could not have sent him to the place He could best work through him to fulfill God's mission. God often has to move us out of our comfort zones to serve Him better.

Following God's guidance always demands a willingness to deny yourself, take up your cross daily, and follow Christ (Luke 9:23). When God beckons you to leave where you are and go anywhere He leads, make your obedience immediate and absolute. You can't just sit where you are if God invites you to be on mission with Him.

Spiritual Marker #6: God guides you on His mission for His glory. God used many means to guide David. God was willing to show him step by step as he followed Him obediently. David's heart was so in tune with God that He could guide him on His mission (2 Sam. 11:2–10).

One of the evidences that the Bible is true is that it reveals the weaknesses and failures of its heroes. Failure comes from not following God's guidance. One Bible passage describes a time when

107

David did not follow God's guidance and instead followed his own lusts. In this familiar circumstance:

- David should have been leading his army instead of remaining home.
- He should have looked at the stars and worshiped God (Ps. 19) instead of watching Bathsheba bathe.
- He should have been thanking God for His goodness instead of forgetting his covenant with God and thus falling into adultery with Bathsheba and then engineering the murder of her husband, Uriah.

How many times I have wished David had let God guide him that night! How often I have lamented that he gave the enemies of the Lord a chance to blaspheme his God instead of bringing glory to God. If I, as a student of Scripture, have felt this way, how much more God, and eventually David, regretted not listening to God and following His guidance!

Do you find yourself being drawn into temptation? Today Satan makes pornographic material readily available on television, the Internet, and other places. Becoming involved in an illicit sexual relationship seems much easier and more acceptable. The greatest protection is a love relationship with God and a strict adherence to His command to flee "evil desires" (2 Tim. 2:22 NIV).

It helps to realize anyone can fall if he or she doesn't depend on God. As a young preacher, I remember reading David's story and thinking, *I'd never do anything like that.* Dr. Herschel Hobbs, a renowned Christian leader, once took some of us young "preacher boys" aside and told us about a pastor who had fallen. Then

Dr. Hobbs shocked me by saying, "I can't say that that won't ever happen to me. The heart is deceitful above all things and desperately wicked. Who can know it? First Corinthians 10:12–13 says, 'So, if you think you are standing firm, be careful that you don't fall! No temptation has seized you except what is common to man. And God is faithful; he will not let you be tempted beyond what you can bear. But when you are tempted, he will also provide a way out so that you can stand up under it'" (NIV).

I couldn't believe my ears. How could such a mighty leader admit—especially in public—that he might fall! Many times since then I have thanked God for Dr. Hobbs's openness. He helped me realize that if I thought I was strong enough to resist temptation on my own, I was vulnerable. His honesty with people as well as God's hand on him may well have been what kept Herschel Hobbs faithful to the end of his life—some forty years after he made that comment.

Are you aware of the ways Satan has tempted you or is able to tempt you to fall? It is crucial that you identify these areas, be honest with God about them, and work out ways to protect yourself from Satan's snares. For some the problem is arrogance. For others it is the quest for material possessions. And for still others it may be an addiction of some sort. Addictions come in all sorts of shapes and sizes. It may be to pornography, alcohol, or drugs, but it may also be to work and pleasing others. What's important is to identify where you are most vulnerable, to develop skills and patterns that protect yourself, and to depend fully on God.

God was faithful to convict David of his sin by sending His prophet Nathan. David could have hardened his heart against God, but instead his heart was broken. He repented of his sin and

109

was restored to full fellowship with God. God will always forgive you regardless of the sin (Ps. 32), but at what cost? God stated eight consequences of David's sin that he reaped. Read 2 Samuel 12:11–13; 13:1–15; 15; and 18:32–33 about these eight consequences of David's sin and weep.

When you miss God's guidance, it usually happens because you are not in proper relationship with Him. The key then becomes not how God guides you but how you respond to Him. Forgiveness begins with a repentant heart and includes turning away from whatever the sin is. Ask God to help you repent of any sins you have as David did his sins in Psalm 51. God does not give you a road map of life but a relationship for life. You don't need a road map if you listen to the Maker of the road accompanying you!

Spiritual Marker #7: God uses you to bring glory to His name. God used David in countless ways. David was used in his own day, but today even more people read his writings, especially the psalms where he bared his soul, than that of any other author.

God used David to establish His kingdom, to unify His people, to establish worship, and to prepare for the temple to be built, as well as in many other ways. You may not have the same gifts David had, but if you have a willing heart that is in intimate fellowship with God, He will use you on mission with Him to bring great glory to His name!

When David killed Goliath, his skill with the slingshot was not nearly so important as was his heart to glorify God and make Him known among the nations. When he later wrote and sang psalms, his ability to compose songs and play the harp again was not nearly so important as was his open heart to God and others to express his deepest feelings.

If David had lacked the musical ability to compose and play songs, they might not have been preserved. But what makes them so precious to millions of people is that David was able to open his heart to God and to people and let us see his deepest feelings in the midst of trials and temptations—in confession and in worship. God used him to give us a timeless message of hope and abiding faith! Pray continuously that God will make you also a man or woman after God's own heart—one who seeks God's glory more than anything else in life.

DAVID'S 180-DEGREE CORPORATE EXPERIENCE WITH THE SPIRITUAL MARKERS

Never lose sight of the fact that God's plan includes His people's reigning with Him. No one lives or dies to himself or herself. You influence the people around you for good or bad. Like a pebble thrown into a lake, your life will ripple out to touch distant shores. God used David to change His people corporately through the same Spiritual Markers He had used in David's life.

Corporate Spiritual Marker #1: God chooses His people as His instruments to reach the world. God took the human concept of kingdom that people understood and used it to help Israel see that He alone is King of kings and that they should obey Him. He took their limited concept of kingdom and expanded it to include the whole world.

David and his son Solomon were part of God's plan to teach Israel about Himself and His kingdom. However, the Israelites mistook God's choice of them for His approval and equated their earthly kingdom with God's eternal kingdom. They saw themselves as God's chosen reservoir of God's grace to which the rest of the world must come rather than the river of God's grace that flows to the world.

Because Israel failed to understand their role in establishing God's kingdom, God destroyed her earthly power. The exile in Babylon was a seventy-year object lesson to teach Israel that God alone is God and that she must obey Him.

Unfortunately, even then Israel learned the wrong lesson. Instead of returning to the personal relationship, Israel's faith turned to legalism. By New Testament times—over four hundred years later—the Law itself was hardened into a legalistic mold, and the concept of Israel as God's favored people had narrowed to shut out the rest of the peoples of the world. Other peoples were not allowed to worship God unless they became Jews. Israel perverted her responsibility for the nations by presuming that she alone was the object of God's love.

God's people today often make the same mistake Israel made. We try to shape ourselves to reflect the world rather than proclaiming the kingdom of God to the world. When this happens, churches either close down, linger on the brink of death, or mask their problems with a high level of social activity. God's plan is for churches to be houses of prayer for all peoples to reconcile a lost world to Him.

What evidence is your church demonstrating that it is being used to fulfill its calling to reconcile the lost of this world to God? If you are striving to be on mission with God, your church also must be moving in the same direction He is moving. Certainly it should not be moving in the opposite direction! You can exert influence to lead your church to be on mission with God.

As you look around you, note whether your church is sponsoring mission trips to places and people groups that need to hear the gospel proclaimed, both overseas and nearer home. Be alert to whether these trips are social occasions or truly opportunities to share the gospel.

Corporate Spiritual Marker #2: God calls all His people to be on mission with Him. God called Israel out of Egypt, delivering her people and establishing them so they would follow Him and worship Him. When they rejected Him and asked for a king like other nations around them, God accommodated and gave them Saul. Samuel was crushed that the people of Israel had rejected the Lord as their king (1 Sam. 8:4–9).

Although God warned Israel what having an earthly king would be like, He had David waiting in the wings to lead them in the paths of righteousness. The Lord was not caught by surprise when Saul, the people's choice, failed. God planned to raise up a king who would be a "man after my own heart," who would reveal Himself and His purposes to the world.

Throughout history God has called out leaders to redirect His people when they have gone astray. In dark and decadent times He raised up leaders such as Martin Luther, Jonathan Edwards, George Whitefield, Charles Finney, and John and Charles Wesley, who had a vibrant, intimate relationship with Him, to stir revivals and spiritual awakenings. Is it possible you might be such a leader?

Today He is again calling His church to follow Him instead of imitating Israel, who rejected Him as their leader. He longs for a close, intimate fellowship with His children. He desires that we live in unity under His leadership. The Lord also wants us to share the good news of the gospel throughout the world—not grasping greedily a special relationship with Him for our own personal benefit, as Israel did. Is it possible that God is calling your church to become an on-mission-with-God congregation?

To answer that question, start by observing how well God's people in your church are following Christ as king. Be sensitive to the spiritual atmosphere in your church. Beyond being just a nice social community, note whether your church is experiencing a continual outpouring of God's Spirit in renewal. If not, what can you do to help bring about that spiritual awakening? Remember also, that every church is called to a specific ministry to further the kingdom. Try to discern what role you think God has called your church to play.

Corporate Spiritual Marker #3: God initiates a covenant of promise and obedience with His people that will bless the nations. More than anything else, God wanted His people to love and worship Him. Soon after they arrived in the promised land, the children of Israel forgot their covenant with God to be a holy, separate nation and wanted a king like the other nations. Even this extreme act of defiance did not thwart God's ultimate purpose. He chose David and made a covenant with him to establish His kingdom forever. David demonstrated patience and perseverance before he came to the promised throne. Finally, after the death of Saul, the Lord led David to settle in Hebron, where his own tribe, Judah, covenanted together with him as king to rule over them (1 Chron. 11:1–3). David was so sure of God's covenant with him that he stood firm under incredibly difficult circumstances.

Under David, God graciously gave Israel another opportunity to return to Him and to respond in obedience to the covenant relationship He desired. David reminded Israel of the special status as God's people and of their obligation to obey Him and be His instrument to the nations. He returned the ark of the covenant to Jerusalem and established worship of God there, setting an enthusiastic personal example in public. Later he gathered the materials for a magnificent temple that his son would build. He also put in place the musicians and instruments to be used in the temple worship. He even planned the court of the Gentiles. Later, Jesus, who descended from David's line, would cleanse the temple because Israel had again thwarted His purpose for it (Mark 11:15–18).

Jesus was incensed that the temple dedicated to prayer would become a market of thieves, cheating poor worshipers who had to buy temple sacrifices at inflated prices. He also was angry because the temple was intended to be a house of prayer for all nations, but Israel was treating it as though certain people owned it and could do whatever they wanted. God's covenant with Israel and His kingdom always included all the peoples of the world.

In light of this passage, evaluate your church and its fulfilling of God's covenant with the nations. Is it dedicated to the nations? Or is it consumed with itself?

Corporate Spiritual Marker #4: God prepares His people for their mission. God shaped David to be like Him and to respond as He would. David spent his lifetime preparing God's people to worship and serve Him. Likewise God shapes various components of the corporate body of Christ for His purpose. When churches go through severe trials and distress, God is able to develop perseverance in the church's character.

When I served as president of the Indonesian Baptist Theological Seminary, we discontinued the campus program, which was not producing pastors willing to return to the villages, and redeployed the professors out to the edge of the church-planting movement in the rural areas where most of the people lived and where revival was spreading rapidly. Many alumni opposed discontinuing the campus program. We experienced several years of trials in establishing the new approach.

One day I told God, "I can't take the pressure any more. If one more thing happens, that's it!" The Lord led me to Jeremiah 12:5: "If you have raced with men on foot and they have worn you out, how can you compete with horses? If you stumble in safe country, how will you manage in the thickets by the Jordan?" When I read that verse, I said, "Oh, Lord, you don't mean it's going to get worse?" "Yes," He answered. "You must learn to take a lot more than this if you are going to be ready for what I want to do with you in the future!"

Although distressed because God told me I would face greater problems, I took courage because I realized God was preparing to use me in much greater responsibilities if I would develop perseverance.

Can you recall a time when your church has persevered in difficult circumstances, a testing time through which God has prepared it for greater usefulness? If so, reflect on that experience in light of what you just finished reading.

Corporate Spiritual Marker #5: God sends His people to the place where He can best work through them to accomplish His mission. Once David became king of all Israel, he worked to unite the kingdom in order to honor God. One of the first things he did was attack Jebus, a city on Mount Moriah, where Abraham had gone to sacrifice Isaac. David and his army captured the city and made it the capital of his kingdom, naming it Jerusalem, also known as Zion.

Jerusalem was perfectly situated between the northern and southern tribes of Israel, making it an important unifying center in the nation. It would later be the site of the beautiful temple Solomon built at the Lord's instruction. To it the queen of Sheba would come to determine whether the city and temple were all they were reported to be and would be overwhelmed at all she saw (2 Chron. 9:3–4). Like a magnet Jerusalem attracted rulers of other nations to come and see what the Lord had done for His people and to experience His glory. David expressed why Jerusalem was important in God's scheme in Psalm 122.

Today God places His people in strategic places around the world where He desires His name to be glorified. Missionaries and other Christian workers are making thrusts into populous "gateway cities." These are exciting days on the "last frontier" of missions, days when Christ's body, the church, is being stirred to go to the places where God can work through His people! Missionaries are segmenting cities like Mexico City into clusters of a million persons each and asking United States churches to take responsibility for individual segments because they cannot get to them with the present number of missionaries. Other missionaries are enlisting churches in the United States to partner with local churches in South America to reach unreached people groups of less than twenty-five thousand that have no missionaries. Advocates are seeking churches to adopt the 150 cities in China, each with more than a million people.

If David had preferred to stay with his father in Bethlehem, he would never have established what God desired in Jerusalem. You may have been born in the country or in a small town and not care much for the cities. In 1950, less than 30 percent of the world's people lived in cities. At the beginning of the twenty-first century almost half live there, and by 2025, two-thirds will be urban inhabitants. Already over 70 percent of the people of Latin America live in cities.

New opportunities exist today for reaching these world-class cities. For instance, Christian business people have unprecedented possibilities to be on mission with God to these cities while continuing to live and work mostly in their current places. For example, some business people from a church I know recently visited a large, unreached city in China. While discussing business opportunities there, these Christian business people also surveyed how they and others might make an impact for Christ among the people in that city. Reaching these megacities does not even require going overseas. I know several churches that have sent mission teams to the ghettos of New York.

Corporate Spiritual Marker #6: God guides His people as they go on mission with Him. A believer cannot experience God in all the dimensions God has for him or her apart from the body of Christ. Henry explains it this way: "Something is different about the way a church comes to know God's will and the way an individual knows God's will. A church is the body of Christ. A body

118

functions as one unit with many members. All the members are interdependent; they need one another. No one individual can know all of God's will for a local church. Each member of the body needs the other members of the body to know God's will fully."

Henry includes a clear illustration from *Experiencing God* of how the parts of the body of Christ work together, even as the parts of the human body work together.

"Suppose your eye could say to your body, 'Let us walk down these train tracks. The way is all clear. Not a train is in sight.' So you begin to walk down the tracks.

"Then suppose your ear says to the body, 'I hear a whistle coming from the other direction.'

"Your eye argues, 'But nothing is on the track as far as I can see. Let's keep on walking.' So your body listens only to your eye and keeps on walking.

"Soon your ear says, 'That whistle is getting louder and closer!'

"Then your feet say, 'We can feel the rumbling motion of a train coming.' You had better get your whole body off these tracks."

Even before the church came into existence, David grasped this concept for the people of Israel. He understood both the beauty of the one-to-one relationship believers have with God, and at the same time he knew the importance of corporate worship. How would you respond if you encountered persons who maintained they don't need a church to worship God?

Corporate Spiritual Marker #7: God uses His corporate people to fulfill His mission. God's promises to David were certainly fulfilled as He used him in a remarkable way during his lifetime. The apostle Paul later commented, "For David, after serving his own generation in God's plan, fell asleep" (Acts 13:36). What an epitaph! It emphasizes a fact that you can overlook: you can only serve your own generation! God can multiply that service in the future, but not if you don't do what you can in your generation.

As a young man David would never have guessed how God would use his life to impact not only his own generation but also generations afterward. Today God desires to use you and His corporate body to fulfill His mission in the world. When David realized all God was planning to do through him, he prayed the prayer found in 2 Samuel 7:8–22 that I would encourage you to read now.

Here are some practical ways God can use your church to fulfill His mission in the world.

- Adopt a single missionary or couple—praying for them, communicating with them, supporting them with various resources.
- Give to special offerings to minister to the peoples of the world.
- Present programs to make people more aware of needs around the world.
- Create special ministries to society's down-and-out, such as crisis pregnancy centers, prison ministries, and pro grams for the homeless.
- Work in the inner city.
- Send youth on missions.

THE 360-DEGREE ETERNAL PERSPECTIVE

God not only worked in the lives of David and of Israel to reveal His glory and His mission, but He communicated to everyone for all time His reign's eternal nature. God revealed through David that He was establishing His kingdom that would have no end and that His kingdom would surpass all kingdoms of this world.

Here are four eternal revelations about the kingdom of God that God showed David and that He wants us to practice today.

Eternal Revelation #1: The kingdom is the reign of the sovereign Lord in the lives of His people, and through them He extends His rule to the world. Throughout the universe, God is in complete control (Pss. 10:16; 103:19). An accurate view of His sovereignty is the bedrock of a proper perspective on His kingdom. The Scripture says that all peoples will bow down to the Lord, who will rule over them (Ps. 22:27–8); the saints will tell of the glory of God's everlasting kingdom (Ps. 145:10–13); they will participate in establishing the everlasting kingdom where all rulers will worship and obey God (Dan. 7:27); and God will make it possible for all nations to hear the proclamation of the gospel, believe, obey, and glorify Him (Rom. 16:25–27).

Has God abdicated His throne because of the universal rebellion of the human race? Not a chance! Instead, He works to redeem the human race and restore His rule. David's kingship began the unfolding of His plan to restore God's kingdom to its right place in the hearts of people.

Eternal Revelation #2: The kingdom is a discipling movement of God that brings total devotion and obedience to the will of God among His people. God chose Abraham to be the father of a nation that was to be God's peculiar people and through which He would bless all nations. God used Moses to show the principles of His righteous rule of His people. Then God raised up David to be king to further reveal His sovereignty. With each, God instituted a critical element in His eventual reign. God used Abraham to establish faith as the basic means of relating to Him and obeying Him. He used Moses to establish obedience to the Law as an indication of how His kingdom was to function. He used David to establish worship as the response to His sovereignty as Lord over all.

God used each of the three persons you have studied so far to disciple His people and to establish an ideal for the kingdom. Through Abraham, God taught us the value of faith. Through Moses, He showed us the importance of obedience to God's law, and through David He illustrated the necessity of the worship of God as Sovereign over all.

During David's lifetime, God promised him a kingdom without end. Through the prophets God also showed that David's offspring would be the One to restore the kingdom and reign and rule over it. The Davidic dynasty was designed to further God's mission in His world. Jesus took the promises that were related to David (Rev. 5:5; 22:16). Revelation reveals the triumphant One to be "the Lion from the tribe of Judah, the Root of David" (Rev. 5:5). Jesus says of Himself, "I am the Root and the Offspring of David, the Bright Morning Star" (Rev. 22:16). Could David, who started out as a nobody, have looked down the centuries of time, he would have been amazed at the way God used his life. Not only was his leadership crucial in his lifetime, but the Lord would bless his life eternally by making him the

122

ancestor of God's only begotten Son! God is preparing His people for His kingdom. You would be amazed at how God intends to use your life to help establish His eternal kingdom.

Eternal Revelation #3: The kingdom is the pressing reality of God's presence impacting every person and everything in the world through His Son Jesus Christ. Matthew 1:1 begins the New Testament by tracing Christ to David and Abraham, the two key figures from whose seed would come the Messiah: "The historical record of Jesus Christ, the Son of David, the Son of Abraham." God arranged it so that Jesus was born in David's birthplace—Bethlehem. People referred to Christ as "the Son of David."

The pressing reality of God's presence was experienced when Jesus came announcing the kingdom and calling on people to repent. He summed up His mission and God's purpose in that one phrase—the kingdom of God. The kingdom arrived when the king appeared. The king begins to reign in people's hearts when they accept Him. It continues to spread each time someone believes the gospel. It will culminate when every knee bows and every tongue confesses Jesus as Lord.

God alone establishes His kingdom. He has done His part up to now and is ready to finish the job. However, He gives you every chance to partner with Him. He wants you to reign with Him someday. The time of Christ's coming and complete victory is hidden from you so you will be about your Father's business always. You have had the gospel revealed to you so that you can reveal it to the world before judgment day.

As a disciple of Christ, be conscious that you are a part of the kingdom of God. Let it dominate your thoughts and actions.

When asked to make a decision, think of the kingdom. When something unusual happens, think of the kingdom. During your daily activities, think of the kingdom. Jesus said, "From the days of John the Baptist until now, the kingdom of heaven has been suffering violence, and the violent have been seizing it by force" (Matt 11:12).

Eternal Revelation #4: The kingdom is the mission of God that culminates in Christ's victory in the world to the glory of God. Christ's kingdom came humbly and unobtrusively, bringing the miracle of spiritual life and the blessings of God's rule in the hearts of people. The blessings of the coming age are with you now in the presence of God all around you. God's kingdom moves forward as Jesus' disciples take the gospel into the entire world.

Jesus told the unbelieving Jews, "The kingdom of God will be taken away from you and given to a nation producing its fruit" (Matt. 21:43). Christ's church became the "holy nation" (1 Pet. 2:9). God's redemptive purpose in history is now being worked out through His corporate body, the church. The conflict still rages, but as God's people carry the gospel of the kingdom into the entire world, the kingdom of Satan is being assaulted and thrown down.

God has entrusted you with a part of continuing and consummating that task! Your responsibility is to be faithful as He completes it. The kingdom's urgency relates both to the impending judgment of God on people's sin and the promise that God will deal in mercy with those who believe in Him. You have only two alternatives to the kingdom tension: (1) give up all hope and responsibility for this world, retire from it, and let it go its suicidal way to hell; or (2) by aggressive witness fulfill your stewardship in God's establishing of the kingdom.

You are part of a generation of priests chosen to reign with the king. If you are to reign with Christ in the coming kingdom, you must serve during its rise to power.

5

JESUS ON MISSION WITH GOD

A SAVIOR FOR ALL PEOPLES

"The Word became flesh
and took up residence among us.
We observed His glory,
the glory as the only Son from the Father,
full of grace and truth."

—John 1:14

EACH SATURDAY DURING MY FIRST FULL YEAR OF MISSIONARY SERVICE after a year of language study, I read to my Moslem secretary the sermon I had composed in Indonesian to see if it was grammatically correct and understandable before I preached it on Sunday. More often it was the concepts, not the language, that were difficult for her to understand.

One day as I read her a message I remarked offhandedly, "I love God."

She responded: "How do you love God? I don't love God."

I told her, "I love God because He first loved me. Why don't you love God?"

She said, "I am afraid of Him because of my sins."

I then told her, "I love God because He sent His Son to save me. If I didn't love Him, I would not be in Indonesia."

"But how can I love Him? We have no *penjelmaan*," she exclaimed.

"I am so glad you used that word *penjelmaan*," I answered. "That is the Indonesian word for *incarnation*. Oh, now I understand why you can't love God. If God had not come in Jesus Christ, I could not love Him either. But since He first loved me and sent His Son, it's easy to love Him."

A little later we got into a dialogue about the crucifixion. I told her, "Christ died for you."

"But He didn't die for me," she replied. "He died for Christians."

"No," I said, "He died for you. He died for everyone."

"But we do not accept Him," she said.

"Nevertheless, He died for you anyway. What a shame that you don't receive Him," I said.

"But why did He have to die?" she asked.

I replied, "Because no other way existed for a person to be saved. If any other way existed, Jesus would not have died. The night before the crucifixion, He asked the Father if there was any other way, but there wasn't. Jesus said, "'I am the way, the truth, and the life. No one comes to the Father except through Me'" (John 14:6).

Just as Mount Everest towers above the mountains surrounding it, so the life of the Lord Jesus Christ towers above all other persons who have ever lived. The glory of God is 100 percent present in Jesus, 100 percent of the time. That does not mean that Jesus radiated glory all the time, as He did on the mount of transfiguration. He manifested God's presence many ways. Jesus manifested God's glory in His character, His attitude, His teachings, His actions, and His ways. Jesus said, "The one who has seen Me has seen the Father" (John 14:9). Through His only begotten Son, God revealed His love and His purpose to reconcile the world to Himself. Jesus is the pattern for our lives.

When we discussed which persons in the Bible were the most significant in revealing God's mission, Henry and I debated whether to include Jesus in this book. That may sound preposterous to you, but He is unique and has no weakness, unlike all the other characters. We asked ourselves, *Did Jesus experience the Seven Realities that we have seen the other characters experience?* Yes, He did, though as the unique Son of God there were, no doubt, some differences. Actually we had no choice. How can you talk about light without the sun or life without the Life-giver, or God without the exact representation of His being? (Heb. 1:3). Jesus is the centerpiece of God's mission, and through Him we experience God in His glory.

A CLOSE-UP VIEW OF JESUS EXPERIENCING THE SEVEN REALITIES

Reality #1: God is always at work around you. God was always at work around Jesus all His life (John 5:16–17). Think about how you announced the birth of your child or would

129

announce it if you had a child. Some people send engraved announcements. Others display banners. Some publish special newspapers. How did God announce the coming of His Son?

God revealed His glory as He prepared for His Son's arrival. He was busy working throughout Old Testament times to foretell and prepare for His Son's arrival on earth. He foretold that Jesus would be born in Bethlehem (Mic. 5:2), that He would come out of Egypt (Hos. 11:1), and that He would be from Nazareth (Matt. 2:23). (Think about how the scribes and Pharisees must have tried to explain that prophecy about where He came from! Even then they would have missed His true place of origin.) An angel was sent to Mary to tell her she would be Christ's mother. The Father sent a dream to Joseph to announce Jesus' name and tell about His work of saving His people from their sins. An angelic choir gave glory to God as it announced Jesus' birth to simple shepherds. A bright star guided wise men from the East to where Jesus was. An angel told Joseph to flee to Egypt so Herod couldn't kill Jesus. Another angel was sent to tell Joseph when to return to Nazareth.

God was certainly busy getting ready for this earthshaking event, announcing it to all concerned and guiding explicitly its every detail!

In her first meeting with the angel, Mary learned Jesus would be born of a virgin, would be named Jesus, would be called the Son of the Most High, would reign as the Son of David forever, and would be called the Son of God (Luke 1:26–38). No doubt she shared these facts with her growing Son. Not much is told about the childhood years of Jesus.

The next glimpse we see of Jesus in Scripture is at age twelve, when sons normally accompanied their parents on their annual trip to Jerusalem for the Passover. He lingered in the temple at Jerusalem for three days before Mary and Joseph realized He was not with them (Luke 2:41–52). As Jesus sat, listened, and asked questions, the people were amazed at Him. Jesus' words to His anxious earthly parents show a remarkable awareness of His involvement in the Father's work in the world. Although He was doing His Father's work, notice that He went back to Nazareth and obeyed His parents. Luke 2:52 reports He also grew in wisdom (mentally), in stature (physically), and in favor with God (spiritually) and with others (socially). What a wonderful pattern for us!

From our earliest days of learning about God, we have experienced God at work around us. Perhaps as a child in Sunday school singing "Jesus loves me, this I know," you became aware of God's being at work through Jesus. Or perhaps you were like Paul who, as an adult, became aware of God's work in Christ. All of us who know Christ can recall the time when we experienced Him working in our lives and first realized He has a purpose for our lives.

Sadly, almost one of every three people in the world has never heard of Christ. The good news has never been shared with them. There are at least six times more people in the world who don't know Christ today than when He gave the Great Commission. Nevertheless, He is the light for every person in the world (John 1:9). He invites us to help finish His work by telling people around the world about God's great love for them!

Reality #2: God pursues a continuing love relationship with you that is real and personal. The Son of God was always aware that the Father loved Him. Jesus announced that the Father showed Him everything He does (John 5:20). Jesus revealed the Father and His love to the disciples (John 17:26). Jesus asked the Father to show His disciples His relationship with the Father before creation (John 17:24). Jesus basked in His Father's love.

You can know that the Lord loves you because of what He did for you on the cross (Rom. 5:8). You have felt His presence as He revealed Himself to you and drew you to Himself. He has communicated His love to you through persons who know Him and who introduced Him to you. If you have not yet had a personal experience with God through Christ, you can be sure that He is pursuing you even as you read this. Even if you know Him as well as the disciples did, He has more of Himself that He wants to reveal to you.

Reality #3: God invites you to become involved with Him in His work. Before the world was created, the Father invited Jesus to be involved in His work (John 1:1–3). At age thirty, He knew what that work entailed and was ready to embark on His public ministry with all of His might and zeal. At His baptism the Father declared His approval of His Son when the Spirit of God descended like a dove on Him and God said, "This is My beloved Son. I take delight in Him!" (Matt. 3:16–17).

Every revelation of God and every assurance of His love are invitations from God. He beckons you to join Him. When did God last speak to you through Scripture? Did you recognize that He spoke to you to involve you in His mission, or did you just think it was a nice devotional thought? Stop and reread that

Scripture. Ask God why He spoke to you and what it could have to do with your joining Him in His mission.

Reality #4: God speaks by the Holy Spirit through the Bible, prayer, and circumstances to reveal Himself, His purposes, and His ways. Although Jesus constantly communicated with the Father, God still used the same ways to speak to Him as He does to you. The Father spoke directly to Him through the Holy Spirit, who communicated to Jesus without limits (John 3:34). Jesus listened intently to the Father and limited His teaching to what He heard (John 5:20; 14:10).

Wouldn't you like to know that the words you hear and speak are from God? This can be your experience! Although you may not have the continual, perfect communication that Jesus did with the Father, Jesus promised in John 16:13, "When the Spirit of truth comes, He will guide you into all truth. For He will not speak on His own, but He will speak whatever He hears. He will also declare to you what is to come." God uses the same methods to speak to you that He used to speak to Jesus.

First, the Father spoke to Jesus through the Bible. Jesus often said that what He did was the fulfillment of Scripture. The Father spoke directly to Jesus through the Scriptures. Today He does the same with you.

Second, the Father spoke to Jesus through prayer. Jesus' prayer life was so compelling that His disciples asked Him to teach them to pray (Luke 11:1–4). His communication with His Father came to a heart-rending culmination as Jesus prayed in the garden of Gethsemane (Matt. 26:36–46). Again, on the cross, Jesus cried out to His Father.

Third, the Father spoke to Jesus through circumstances. In the midst of the circumstances surrounding Him, Jesus realized the Father was at work. He joined Him immediately. Thus, when He was teaching John's disciples, He responded to the dilemma of Jairus, a synagogue ruler whose daughter was dying (Matt. 9:18–25). On the way to solve Jairus's problem, He realized that the Father was at work inspiring faith in the woman who touched the hem of His robe. He stopped and redirected His attention to the woman with the issue of blood. He healed and released her from this plague, which had rendered her unclean for twelve long years! He knew that when He joined the Father at work in that moment the Father would provide what He needed when He arrived at Jairus's house. Sure enough Jairus's daughter was dead. Jesus prayed for the Father to raise her from the dead, and He did.

How often are you so focused on one thing that God is doing that you miss an opportunity God is presenting you through other circumstances? I have discovered that interruptions are often divine appointments.

On another day when Jesus passed through Jericho, He looked up in a tree and saw Zacchaeus. He knew that the Father was at work because no one seeks to know Christ without the Father's prompting. Whenever you see someone wanting to know more about Christ, realize that God is waving a red flag for you to interrupt your schedule and join Him on mission. Jesus threw away His DayTimer and went to lunch with Zacchaeus. That day Zacchaeus became a true son of Abraham even though he was a publican (Luke 19:1–10). Be so attuned to the Spirit of God that you recognize the circumstances where God is at work around you and immediately join Him!

Reality #5: God's invitation for you to work with Him always leads you to a crisis of belief that requires faith and action. We may have difficulty understanding the faith that Jesus exercised because we tend to concentrate on His divine nature more than His human nature. I believe Jesus did His miracles by faith (Heb. 12:2). Jesus believed the Father was leading Him throughout His earthly ministry and, without once wavering, was willing to do what He asked. In His final act of trust in God, He faced death with faith that the Spirit would resurrect Him. When you face a crisis of faith, realize that Jesus is your model. He lived by faith and acted completely by faith.

Reality #6: You must make major adjustments in your life to join God in what He is doing. You may think that because Jesus was God's Son, He didn't have to make major adjustments when the Father revealed His will to Him. The opposite is true.

The Son of God was willing to put His desires aside and adjust to the Father's will as He emptied the bitter cup for you and me and all the peoples of the world (Matt. 26:37–43). In your culture, geared to creature comforts, you must battle constantly against the day's currents. Willingness to make the kind of adjustments Jesus did will be worked into your character only as you surrender obediently to the Father and allow His Holy Spirit to transform you into Christ's image.

The Lord requires major adjustments from you to bring yourself in line with His will. Even as you follow Him day by day, you will often be surprised at the direction in which He wants to lead you. He may require an adjustment in what you are doing or how you are doing it. Often a major change in attitude is required. As you reflect on the invitation He extends to you, look at the faith step He asks you to make. Realize that if you don't make it, you will not be able to join Him in what He wants you to do next for His kingdom and personally to experience Him.

Reality #7: You experience God's glory as you obey Him and He accomplishes His work through you. The Bible clearly reveals that Jesus learned obedience by the things that He experienced in His brief lifetime on earth (Heb. 5:7–9).

Not only did He learn by experience, but He also suffered temptations during His life so He can help those who are being tempted (Heb. 2:18). He "has been tested in every way as we are, yet without sin" (Heb. 4:15). The Son of God lived a perfect life on this earth and then tasted death for every person—you and me and everyone else.

Jesus lived thirty-three years—not a long life by today's standards. In that short span of time, however, He finished the work the Father gave Him to do. His final words on the cross were, "It is finished!" (John 19:30). In His final hours on earth, Jesus said, "I have glorified You on the earth by completing the work You gave Me to do" (John 17:4).

You have no idea how long God has given you to live on this earth. Only the Lord knows the total plan for your life. As you seek to align your life with God's mission, realize you will be enabled to experience God all your life by following the lessons you learn from the life of Jesus. As you review how the Father used Jesus and worked through His entire life to accomplish His mission, ask God to reveal how He wants your whole life to accomplish His mission.

THE WIDE-ANGLE VIEW OF JESUS' LIFETIME

We think of Jesus from a lifetime perspective subconsciously. His whole life has so impacted us and the world that each time we see Him experiencing the Father we think of it as just one more example of His total life. Yet the Father used the same process with Him that He uses with us. He experienced the Seven Spiritual Markers as we do.

Spiritual Marker #1: God chooses you to be on mission with Him to reconcile a lost world to Himself. Peter declares that Jesus "was destined before the foundation of the world, but was revealed at the end of the times for you" (1 Pet. 1:20). Thousands of years before it occurred, the Father promised to answer the Son's request to give Him the nations as His inheritance and the ends of the earth as His possession (Ps. 2:7–8).

God not only chose Jesus but also chose you, before the world's foundation (Eph. 1:4, 11). How reassuring to realize God planned your life before the creation of the world! God's initiative in calling you to Him was not a spur-of-the-moment decision. Neither did you take the initiative to choose Him. You may not understand how He chose you before you were born, but once you are in the kingdom of God, He reveals that He made the initial choice. That means He has a purpose to fulfill in you (Jer. 1:4–9).

Spiritual Marker #2: God calls you to accompany Him on His mission. The Father's calling of Jesus is an important concept in Scripture. The word *called* is used of Jesus in Matthew 2:15: "Out of Egypt I called My Son." Early in His earthly life, Jesus sensed the Father's call. At the age of twelve, He said He must be about His Father's business.

Jesus also sensed God's call at the time of His baptism and insisted that His cousin John baptize Him. After that encounter with God, Christ sensed the Spirit's call to go into the wilderness for Satan to tempt Him about His call.

Think back on God's call to you. God's call was not only for salvation but also for service. His call to follow Him did not mean just to follow Him down a church aisle or in baptism. His call is to be like Jesus and to let Jesus live His life through you (Luke 9:23).

For too long, many Christians have misunderstood the call and thought only those involved in professional ministry were "called." Every Christian needs to listen carefully for what God is asking him or her to do by faith.

Spiritual Marker #3: God initiates a covenant of promise and obedience with you. Jesus fulfilled all the Old Testament covenants. As Abraham's seed, Jesus fulfilled the prophecy given to Abraham. Galatians 3:16 specifically states: "The promises were spoken to Abraham and to his seed. He does not say 'and to seeds,' as though referring to many, but 'and to your seed,' refer-ring to one, who is Christ." Jesus' primary covenant was with the Father. He was the lamb slain before the foundation of the world. Jesus declared His willingness to fulfill the covenant of redemp-tion by sacrificing Himself for the world's sins to fulfill the Old Covenant and to establish the New Covenant (Heb. 10:8–10).

Christ's awareness of His covenants with the Father and God's covenants with His people kept Him focused on His purpose.

During His earthly life, He operated on the basis of God working through Him to fulfill His mission in the world.

Spiritual Marker #4: God prepares you for His mission. Preparation is an important part of the mission on which God desires to send you. He prepares His servants to be in a position to do His will. Through the struggles you experience in this world, you are prepared to do God's will. The Father prepared Jesus before He came on His mission to redeem the world. But He continued to prepare Jesus throughout His lifetime to fulfill His mission. God's directive that He grow up in a faithful Jewish family helped Him understand the mission. His participation in the rigorous training in the synagogue given young men of His day further prepared Him. His baptism and the Father's loving affirmation prepared Him for the wilderness temptations.

You may marvel that the loving Spirit of God led Jesus into the desert to be tempted. Jesus, the hero of all time, had no weaknesses, but it took the unexpected event of the temptation to prove that point for all eternity! Satan questioned Jesus' identity as the Son of God and dared Him to prove it by changing stones into bread for His own use. Satan also questioned the way Jesus would accomplish His mission and lead people to follow Him and questioned the means by which Jesus would become king over all the kingdoms of the earth (Luke 4:1–13).

Jesus was face-to-face with the devil, but His focus was on God! Quoting words from the Old Testament, Jesus remained true to the Father's revealed will (Deut. 8:3; 6:13; 6:16). Through the power of the Holy Spirit, He resisted Satan's temptation to seduce Him from His Father's purpose.

Perhaps you have struggled in a similar way. You have felt God inviting you to follow Jesus and get involved in His work, but the pull in other directions has been strong. Or Satan may have tempted you to do it for your own benefit, or in your own way, or by your own power, as he tempted Jesus. Your salvation is not only for you but also for God to fulfill His mission to the whole world!

Satan may tempt you in ways similar to those he used to tempt Jesus. He may challenge you to expose yourself to your greatest temptation, or to do a spectacular work that people can see, or to take a shortcut to success in order to obtain everything you want. Be alert to these and other ways he will tempt you, because he will!

Satan continued to test Jesus throughout His earthly existence, even inducing Peter to rebuke Him for predicting He would die (Matt. 16:22). The Gethsemane experience of asking the Father to let this cup of suffering pass further equipped Christ to pay the ultimate price of redemption. All His life He was being equipped to accomplish His mission. When the time came for Him to die, the Son of God did not falter.

Jesus is recruiting an army. He rescued you from the tyrant who has abused you all your life. He enlisted you to join Him to save others from the tyranny of the tempter. He wants you to be aware of His vision for all peoples to know Him (Phil. 1:29). Every revelation of Him is an invitation for you to join His mission.

Each trial you face equips you to accomplish your mission with God. You may not understand why you must go though one more trial when you think you are already prepared for anything. The

Father, however, knows what further character development you need to match the assignment He has for you. If you are facing a test or trial right now, look at it closely to see what it is God wants to teach you through it.

Spiritual Marker #5: God sends you to the place where He can best work through you to accomplish His mission. In the past you may have struggled to know the place God has chosen for you. No question existed as to the place the Father chose for His Son's mission. If He were to totally identify with people, Christ must live among them. The quest required that He come as the lowliest of people—a servant. Following Jesus' example, nothing God asks of you can compare with the sacrifice He made to be in the place God desired (Phil. 2:5–8).

Think of the ways the Father sent Jesus: in humility, poverty, servanthood, obedience, and even death. Is He sending you in any of these ways?

Does it disturb you to see the word *death* in that paragraph? A newly published history of the Nigerian Baptist Convention reminded me of how often missionaries in the nineteenth century faced death overseas. Many died within months of arriving on Africa's shores; those who survived usually lost spouses and children. What an amazing price they paid to follow God's call to the uttermost part of the world at that time! What a thrill it was for me to attend the 150th anniversary of the first missionaries' arrival and hear the announcement that they now have more than one million church members and are sending missionaries themselves!

For God to use you fully, get to the place where He wants to bless others through you. It may be in your same geographical location but in a servant role or in another part of the

141

geographical area surrounding you. It could also be in another job than you are now doing. But it could be to another people/racial group than your own or to another people group or country where the gospel isn't known.

Spiritual Marker #6: God guides you to join Him on mission. The Father always guided Jesus to do what He desired. Because He loved the Father and had an intimate relationship with Him, Jesus never disappointed Him. The Word He had learned in His youth, prayer in every perplexing situation, and the circumstances in which He found Himself all guided Jesus.

The Father took the initiative and showed Him all that He was doing. For instance, one morning Jesus got up very early while it was still dark. He went off to a solitary place where He prayed (Mark 1:35–38). The disciples expected Him to respond to their announcement that the crowds were looking for Him. Instead Jesus had heard from the Father during His quiet time that He must go to other towns and villages because, "'This is why I have come.'" God's will won out over the appeal of great crowds and others' counsel! Following Jesus' example, be sure you receive your guidance from the Father through the Holy Spirit, rather than just listening to people around you (John 14:18, 26; Matt. 28:20).

Spiritual Marker #7: God uses you to bring glory to His name through His mission. Jesus had the assurance of knowing that He pleased the Father. How the Father must have delighted every day in using Christ to reveal His nature, demonstrate His glory, and accomplish His ultimate purpose in the world! (John 5:30). Because of His obedience and willingness to deny Himself and please the Father, great things were accomplished through His brief life on earth. Satan and death were defeated on the cross, new life was made possible through the resurrection, and victory was assured through His ascension and enthronement. Jesus was able to say at the end of His earthly life that He had glorified the Father (John 17:1–4).

The Lord often surprises you with the next step in the journey. When Jesus told Peter to follow Him and feed His sheep instead of fishing, He revealed that in Peter's old age others would carry him where he did not want to go. Peter tried to shift the subject to someone else, but Jesus told him, "If I want him to remain [alive] until I return, what is that to you? As for you, follow Me" (John 21:22–24). You and I are not to be concerned about how God will use others. He is challenging us with His call to join Him on mission. Don't shift attention to someone else or do what he or she does. Allow the Lord to use you as He chooses!

JESUS' 180-DEGREE EXPERIENCE WITH THE CORPORATE SPIRITUAL MARKERS

Jesus could have won the world by Himself, but He was not content to do that. Instead He realized it was in the Father's plan for Him to establish the church that would take the gospel to the ends of the earth.

Corporate Spiritual Marker #1: God chooses a people to be on mission with Him to reconcile a lost world to Himself. As you have seen, Christ spent much time praying before He selected the twelve disciples. Jesus said that the Father had chosen them beforehand and had given them to Him (John 17:6–10). He took more than three years to teach and train them for the global task. He told His disciples that He was going to build His church on them and their confession of Him as the Son of God (Matt. 16:18–20).

Then after His resurrection, Jesus commissioned them as His church for worldwide mission, saying: "All authority has been given to Me in heaven and on earth. Go, therefore, and make disciples of all nations, baptizing them in the name of the Father and of the Son and of the Holy Spirit, teaching them to observe everything I have commanded you. And remember, I am with you always, to the end of the age" (Matt. 28:18–20).

God has not only chosen you; He has chosen the church—the called-out ones. Everyone in His body is chosen for His purpose. Think about the church where you are a member. What do you believe God's purpose for your church is? Each church is to be a world-missions strategy center. Each church has distinctive local and global roles to play. The game plan has not changed. Just as the disciples were empowered in the first century, the Holy Spirit empowers you and your church in this century to be His witnesses to people in your city, in your state, in your country, and around the globe.

Jesus said that His followers need to carry the gospel to Jerusalem, Judea, Samaria, and the ends of the earth (Acts 1:8). That means your city, your state, your country, and all the other countries of the world. Jesus said that we need to be involved locally as well as globally at the same time. (Remember the new word *glocalization* I mentioned in chapter 1.) Some want to make the order chronological, but Jesus means for us to do all at the same time. Is your church an Acts 1:8 church? Your church can't be so involved in your own neighborhood that it ignores the rest of the world. And at the same time your church can't be so involved overseas that it ignores needs right next door. Johnny Hunt, whose church in the suburbs of Atlanta sends hundreds of volunteers every year around the world, has popularized Oswald Smith's saying in this generation, "The light that shines the farthest shines the brightest at home."

Corporate Spiritual Marker #2: God calls all His people to be on mission with Him. As the Father called Jesus, so He also calls all His people in Christ. God's general call is to be a holy people, a kingdom of priests to the peoples of the world. We have applied the word *call* to individuals so often we miss that it first applied to all the people of God.

Jesus did not give the Great Commission just to the apostles or to a certain class of people. He gave it to every Christian and every church. Some are called to fulfill certain roles in the spreading of the kingdom, but Christ calls all of His followers to be involved in His mission as the body of Christ (Acts 8:4).

Philip went to Samaria, and the Spirit used him to bring multitudes into the kingdom. Next we see him in the desert witnessing to the Ethiopian. God may choose to use you to win the multitudes, but He also wants you and your church to witness to those around you. A church that is truly following the words of Jesus will be witnesses to the world, both far and near. It will have at least one people group on its heart and will be praying for missionaries as well as producing people to be missionaries.

Corporate Spiritual Marker #3: God initiates a covenant of promise and obedience with His people in every generation. Imagine being raised under the rules and regulations of the Old Covenant, then suddenly released to share the glorious freedom of the New Covenant with your generation. This is what the disciples experienced. Through their intimate personal relationship with the Son of God, they underwent a miraculous transformation. These men had to be amazed to be part of a major transition that affected the very roots of their former religion. Instead of sacrificing bulls, goats, and lambs, they now celebrated the New Covenant, in the bread and wine, the broken body and shed blood of Christ, with whom they had walked and talked (Luke 22:14–20). The disciples were excited to tell the world the Lamb of God, whom they knew personally, takes away sins! That same excitement is available today through the New Covenant God has made with you and His church through the blood of His Son.

Corporate Spiritual Marker #4: God prepares His church for His mission. Just as the Father took great pains to prepare His Son for the ministry to which He was called, so Christ carefully prepared His disciples for the work of the kingdom. The Lord spent many hours telling them about the kingdom of God. He used simple parables to drive home the truth. Today, by His Holy Spirit, the Lord is knocking at the door of your church wanting to spend time with you and to prepare your church for an outreach as great as, if not greater than, that of the early apostles. God works through the difficulties you experience to prepare you to be on mission.

God performed miracles in the midst of the first-century church to show He was the One taking the initiative to win the world to Himself. Today on international frontiers we hear about modern-day miracles that God is performing to vindicate His servants and bring people who have never heard the gospel to faith in His Son. Our generation has the opportunity to join God as He reaches out in mighty power to the unreached of our day and age.

Corporate Spiritual Marker #5: God sends His people today to the place where He can best work through them to accomplish His mission. Since Babel (Gen. 11) the world has never been more of a global village than it is today. Migration from all over the world has integrated the peoples of the world. Disasters have dispersed refugees all over the globe. Education has attracted scholars from everywhere to the centers of learning. Historically 20 percent of the future world leaders are studying in the Boston area at any one time. World economics have caused all nations to emphasize learning English as a second language. Business people travel by the millions to other countries.

Why has globalization occurred at this particular time in history? The Greek and Roman civilizations made the possibility of the spread of the gospel to the known world a reality in the first century. Is it possible that God is doing a special work to send us to the nations and the nations to us in order to get the gospel to all people in our day? If so, what do you think God is doing in your life and in your church to get you to the place where He can best work through you to accomplish His mission?

Corporate Spiritual Marker #6: God guides His church to fulfill His mission. For three years the disciples followed Jesus everywhere He went. Their memory bank was full of experiences to which they could refer when they got in trouble. However, Jesus was not willing to leave them to memory. He said that He would send another Counselor, like Himself, who would not only be with them but in them. He would remind them of everything Jesus said and then tell them things Jesus couldn't tell them when

He was on earth, when they were unable to receive His truth. Christ still guides His people who are willing to listen.

The Spirit of Christ guides you into all truth, including that part of the harvest field where God wants you to be. He is responsible for guiding willing and obedient harvesters to the right place. He is free to use any means along the way to be sure you get there. Almost all volunteer, short-term, or career missionaries at home or abroad testify they thought they were going to do one thing, but God had other plans. Believe that God will reveal what He wants you to do when you get to the place where He can best use you in His mission.

Corporate Spiritual Marker #7: God uses His corporate people to fulfill His mission. Jesus demonstrated what it means to be on mission. When Satan, His disciples, His brothers, or His townspeople tried to divert Him, Jesus remained on course because He was always aware of His mission to redeem the lost world. He had a passion to fulfill His mission. Since He believed the results of His mission were sure, He endured whatever it took to finish His task. Help your church adopt that same mind-set today as you rise above the outlook of your affluent culture.

The followers of Jesus wanted to be used of Him, but they only sporadically joined Him on mission often enough to fulfill His purpose. We do see them casting out demons, going on short missionary trips, and ministering to Him. However, we must wait until the next chapter to see them fully being used of Him to accomplish the purpose He gave them in the Great Commission.

JESUS FROM THE 360-DEGREE ETERNAL PERSPECTIVE

From eternity Jesus invaded time. What He did in time impacted eternity. He established the gospel. Paul says the facts of the gospel are Jesus died, was buried, and rose from the dead (1 Cor. 15:3–4). One other fact implied is the incarnation of Christ. When you look at the eternal results of Christ's life, you must focus on His incarnation, crucifixion, and resurrection. Each of these must be believed and acted on for salvation. These facts make Jesus unique in all history. Each makes Jesus the only way to God. No other religion can claim their leader came, died, and rose from the dead for the world's sins. "There is no other name under heaven given to people by which we must be saved" (Acts 4:12).

We will now explore the eternal meaning of God's mission being manifest explicitly through Christ's incarnation, crucifixion, and resurrection for God's mission.

THE INCARNATION

"God has no wife; God has no sex; God has no son," a Moslem friend once said to me vehemently.

"But Mary was not God's wife," I explained. "The Holy Spirit caused a virgin to conceive miraculously. Actually, God became man."

He replied: "God is all-powerful and supremely one. He cannot be three Gods as you Christians teach. He is one. He is all-powerful. He could not become man."

To the Muslim, it is absurd to think that the transcendent, all-powerful God would limit Himself to become a human being. To the Hindu, the distinctiveness of the incarnation as a once-for-all coming of an only true God into history is preposterous. To the Buddhist, for God even to exist is evil. He cannot imagine God becoming a person and living in the world. To the animist, if God is believed in at all, He is far removed from the earth and pays little attention to people and their plight.

No wonder Jesus is the stumbling block to those who will not accept Him as God's revelation. Only God could think up salvation. Man-made religions exalt people to god status; only the Bible teaches God actually became a person.

In Philippians 2:7, the Greek word for "made himself nothing" *(kenoo)* means simply "to empty, to make void or of no effect" (2:7–8 NIV). To be in the form of God means that He was no less God when He took the form of a person. To be in human likeness means that He was no less human because He was God in the flesh. Jesus was not half God and half human but fully God and fully human.

We normally focus on the divine signs at Christ's birth and forget the humanness of it. We are amazed by the virgin birth; we rejoice in the angels' singing; we are awed at the star's appearing; we marvel at the wise men's journey and gifts. But often we fail to realize that He was born in a stable to a woman who conceived before she was married. On that first Christmas night, perhaps Mary thought: *Can this really be the Son of God? It's been nine months since the angel spoke to me. Did I only dream it? If this is truly the Messiah, why are we in a stable? Where is God?*

God could have reassured her, "He is in your lap, Mary . . . as much as He is in heaven." How overwhelming the thought that the God who created all the universe limited Himself to a human form, approximately eighteen inches long and weighing approximately seven pounds! No wonder other religions find believing the incarnation so difficult!

In using the graphic metaphor "He emptied himself," the Bible expresses the completeness of Christ's self-renunciation. Scholars debate what it meant for Christ to empty Himself. Nevertheless, you cannot ignore New Testament evidence that Jesus laid aside His advantages as God to face life as you and I do. His identification with us is complete.

Even though He was the only perfect person who ever lived, Jesus was also human and experienced what it means to be human. Jesus had to grow in wisdom and in physical stature (Luke 2:52). He had to learn obedience. He got angry. He was hungry. He experienced pain. He was thirsty. He lived by faith and prayer. He got tired. He experienced the emotions of anger and compassion; He endured pain. He had to live on faith that He was the Son of God and constantly to resort to the place of prayer to receive the Father's knowledge and wisdom. Yes, Jesus was really human.

Almost as startling as the incarnation was Jesus becoming a servant. A graphic picture of His servant role occurred when Jesus washed His disciples' feet. God, who became a human, stooped to serve people that we might catch the vision of serving.

The uniqueness of Christ's incarnation demands every person in the world know about it. No person's life is complete until he or she has a real-life encounter with the God who invaded history.

151

Jesus, the divine Son, has come in human form, but they don't know it. We Christians cannot rest until all persons know God visited earth to bring them into right relationship with their Creator so they might experience salvation.

THE CRUCIFIXION

The self-emptying of Christ culminated with Gethsemane and Golgotha. Philippians 2:8 moves directly from Christ's incarnation to His crucifixion. Jesus was the Suffering Servant and fulfilled Isaiah's divine prophecies. The cross was unavoidable.

The crucifixion did not catch the Father or the Son by surprise. God did not have to change His plans suddenly. Jesus, the Lamb of God, was slain before the foundation of the world (Rev. 13:8). Since He came to earth for that purpose, He resolutely directed His steps toward Calvary.

In Gethsemane, as the horror of death pressed on Jesus, the Father was His only resource. He enlisted Peter, James, and John to pray for Him, but they slept and left Him to face it alone. The battle of Gethsemane raged. Jesus wanted only to please the Father, but He sought a way to do it other than having to bear the sin of humankind and face death on the cross for every person. No wonder He spoke the words found in Matthew 26:38, "My soul is swallowed up in sorrow—to the point of death. Remain here and stay awake with Me."

The raging battle during the wilderness temptation reached fever pitch in Gethsemane. Satan had assaulted Him at every opportunity. He entered into Peter a short while before. Just after he had confessed that Jesus was the Christ, the Son of the living God, Peter rebuked Jesus for saying He would suffer and die.

Jesus had to say to Peter, "'Get behind Me, Satan! You are an offense to Me because you're not thinking about God's concerns, but man's'" (Matt. 16:23). Satan stopped short of nothing to prevent Jesus from saving us. In Gethsemane Satan assaulted Jesus' humanity to tempt Him to back off from His impending sacrifice. Jesus' human and divine nature seemed to clash.

Jesus was not role-playing. The battle was real. Yet Jesus completely surrendered to the Father's will. Jesus' will, always submissive to the Father's, overcame both the physical reality and Satan's demonic presence when He uttered, "Father, if You are willing, take this cup away from Me—nevertheless, not My will, but Yours, be done" (Luke 22:42). At that moment Jesus won the war of the ages! He arose with a confidence that never wavered in the face of soldiers, suffering, and death. For Him, to know the Father's will was to do it (Phil. 2:8).

Jesus' death was the supreme act of atonement, which in the Old Testament meant the covering of sin through God's own provision. On this basis Jesus reconciled people to God (2 Cor. 5:14–6:2). By His death Jesus satisfied the Father, subdued Satan, and reconciled people to God. Forgiveness was made available to those who believe in Christ as Savior on the basis of His sacrifice.

Since Christ died for the world, every person has a right to choose salvation. People may choose not to respond to Christ's offer, but if they are not given a chance to hear and respond, then we have robbed them of the opportunity that Christ died to give them.

People are lost for only two reasons: first, they have never adequately heard the message of salvation, or, second, they have rejected God's offer of reconciliation in Christ. We cannot do much about the second reason, but we are obliged to eliminate the first reason.

After Satan's attempt to eliminate Christ failed, he tried to convince people that the redemptive acts of Christ are not necessary for salvation. Satan falsely says other ways of salvation exist outside of Christ.

What a paradox! Just at the time of the greatest advance of the gospel in history, Satan's philosophy—now adopted by the postmodern world—has permeated the life-stream of the church and sapped our spiritual strength. Thought patterns growing out of universalism, humanism, and secularism have robbed many Christians of the verve and audacity to proclaim Jesus Christ as Savior and Lord to every person. This insidious, worldly philosophy is daily heard in the following expressions:

- "Other peoples have their own religions; leave them alone."
- "Be tolerant of others and not so bigoted that you tell them that they are wrong if they don't accept Christ as the only way to God."
- "We haven't done so well ourselves; we should clean up our own back doorstep before we go to other nations to tell them how to live."

When we cease to believe that Jesus is the only way of salvation, we disqualify ourselves to be on mission with God. Our task as priests is not to offer a sacrifice for sin but to proclaim the sacrifice that Jesus has made. Our priestly role is to make the cross real to people at the crossroads of their lives.

THE RESURRECTION

Had Jesus stayed in the grave, the incarnation and crucifixion would have been a dead-end street for God's mission. Satan might have appeared to have won the battle if we didn't have the Old Testament prophecies and Jesus' own predictions.

God's counteroffensive, the resurrection, gained the victory. The physical, bodily resurrection of Jesus firmly established God's invasion of history. The empty tomb and His appearances to the believers authenticated it. Jesus actually ate, was touched by, and transformed believers. Jesus' resurrected body was more than His physical body. God's glory shone through Him. He walked through locked doors and disappeared and appeared at will, but He was the same Jesus the disciples had seen, heard, and felt.

When Jesus emerged from the tomb, a new age dawned on the world! Humanity had a new king! Jesus revealed through the resurrection that He had gained all authority in heaven and in earth (Matt. 28:18). He ruled over sin, death, and every created power. He had reconciled the world to God (2 Cor. 5:18–19; Col. 1:20). Jesus' resurrection proved that the evil forces of Satan had been conquered. In His death and resurrection, Jesus "disarmed the rulers and authorities and disgraced them publicly; He triumphed over them by Him" (Col. 2:15).

The decisive battle has been won over Satan. Satan may continue to defeat Christians and to retard kingdom progress, but the outcome is no longer in doubt. You could compare it to a decisive play in a ball game. The game may not be over, but you know who the winner will be.

The greatest creative act of all time was the resurrection of Jesus (Eph. 1:19–21). Its power is manifested most clearly in us in the new birth (2 Cor. 5:17). The resurrection revealed the nature of God. His love, power, presence, and purpose took on added meaning.

The resurrection became the touchstone of gospel proclamation. Before the resurrection the gospel was not preached to the nations because the good news had not all come to pass. The resurrection brought new meaning and glory to the incarnation and death of Christ. Now the whole gospel could be preached and was preached by the first-century Christians, revealing that God had brought salvation to people in Jesus Christ.

The resurrection ushered in the last days. We live between the resurrection and the return of Christ. During these times the gospel is to be preached to all nations (Matt. 24:14).

Today Christians by the thousands are fanning out all over the world to tell this good news to every person on the face of the earth. Every two months I participate in an appointment service for new missionaries who desire to be a part of this great movement of God that continues. I wish I could tell you every one of the testimonies I hear from these committed Christians. You would be amazed at the diversity of their backgrounds, education, ethnicity, and experience, but you would also see a unity in their desire to follow Christ wherever He leads.

The resurrection cut across all national and racial lines to present us with a universal, spiritual, omnipotent, and omnipresent Christ. That's the meaning of John 1:14, "We observed His glory, the glory as the only Son from the Father, full of grace and truth." People of all nations identify with Him and claim Him as their own. The resurrection forced Christianity to break with Judaism. Christ could not be contained by one race.

Christ's resurrection demands worldwide proclamation that "Jesus is Lord!" Jesus gave the Great Commission on the basis of His resurrection. The resurrection is the condition for world missions. It made Jesus the supreme authority in the missionary enterprise.

On five occasions after the resurrection, Jesus gave the Great Commission and stated it differently in each Gospel and Acts. As you finish this chapter about Jesus, stop and read His last commands in Matthew 28:18–20; Mark 16:15; Luke 24:46–49; John 20:21–23; and Acts 1:8. Each variation has a different emphasis, but each spells out a fresh aspect of the Great Commission.

At Pentecost, Peter gave us the message to take to all peoples of the world, "God has made this Jesus, whom you crucified, both Lord and Messiah!'" (Acts 2:36). And Paul summed it all up in Phililippians 2:9–10: "For this reason God also highly exalted Him and gave Him the name that is above every name, so that at the name of Jesus every knee should bow—of those who are in heaven and on earth and under the earth—and every tongue should confess that Jesus Christ is Lord, to the glory of God the Father." Whether they confess Jesus as Lord now and are saved or confess Him at the judgment seat and are still lost forever will depend on what we do with the Great Commission.

The Christ event divides history into two parts—B.C. and A.D. Too many people today live on the other side of Christ. They have never heard the gospel. For them it is still B.C.

6

PETER ON MISSION WITH GOD

A CHURCH FOR ALL PEOPLES

> "And I tell you that you are Peter, and on this
> rock I will build my church, and the gates of Hades
> will not overcome it. I will give you the keys of the
> kingdom of heaven; whatever you bind on earth will
> be bound in heaven, and whatsoever you loose on
> earth will be loosed in heaven."
> —Matthew 16:18–19 (NIV)

GARY HILLYARD WAS PASTOR OF A SMALL CHURCH IN SEATTLE, Washington, when Communism fell in the former Soviet Union in 1989. He and a few church members began praying every day at noon for God to work in their midst. One Sunday they set aside the regular services in order to involve the whole church in a day of prayer. About 2 P.M. the pastor walked to the door and met a man who said, "I'm a Baptist from the Ukraine. Can I worship

159

with you here?" He began bringing other Ukrainians to church. One of them said, "A family who is emigrating from Luganz, Ukraine, owns a six-room house there that we want to give you for mission work."

Gary retorted, "What can I do with a six-room house in the Ukraine?" He offered the house to his denomination's state convention, and their home and international mission boards, but they said they were not the answer to his prayer. He had been studying *Experiencing God*, so he called Henry Blackaby and asked, "What can I do with a six-room house in the Ukraine?" Henry replied, "That's the wrong question. You need to ask, 'What can God do with a six-room house in the Ukraine?' Your church needs to be a world-mission strategy center. Ask God what you should do."

Not many days afterward, Don English, a former schoolmate of Gary's, called to say, "Gary, I believe I've been called to go to the former Soviet Union." They prayed and talked together. Once again, Gary called Henry Blackaby and asked, "What do I do now? Our church can't support a missionary." Henry asked, "Have you asked the people to give?" Gary said, "No, we are just a little church with less than one hundred people. We are poor people. We can't send a missionary." Henry said, "Why don't you pray and then ask them to give what they can?"

So the church prayed, and Gary invited the people to leave money on the front pew to send the Englishes as missionaries. They got enough for a one-way ticket for the Englishes to go to the Ukraine. Don rented a theatre in Lugantz, Ukraine, and in a week had more than two thousand people come to Christ. Over time they were given a school, a camp, and land for a radio station that TransWorld Radio was able to use. Finally Gary Hilliard, the pastor, resigned the church in Washington and went to the Ukraine, where he began to help take care of the new Christians.

What can a little church with some one hundred people do to affect the world? Whatever God can do, He wants to manifest His purpose and glory through every church. "Every church is to be a world missions strategy center."

Gary must have felt like Peter did. More people identify with Peter than with other characters of the Bible. They say, "You know, I feel like this guy." This rugged fisherman couldn't have had any idea of what the Lord had in mind when He first saw him. All his life was spent out on the lake. His salty language matched his occupation!

A CLOSE-UP VIEW OF PETER'S EXPERIENCE WITH THE SEVEN REALITIES

Since we have looked at the Seven Realities for *Experiencing God* with each of the other characters, let's take a quick look at how God used them in the life of Peter.

Reality #1: God is always at work around you, whether or not you see Him. Peter may not have realized all God was doing around him, but he was a seeker for truth. We first meet him and his brother Andrew as disciples of John the Baptist (John 1:35–42). When John said, "Look, the Lamb of God!" (v. 36). Andrew and another of John's disciples immediately followed Jesus. They asked, "Where are you staying?" Jesus invited them to spend the day with Him. After this exhilarating encounter,

Andrew was so excited, he found his brother, Peter, and said, "We have found the Messiah!" (v. 41). He introduced him to Jesus. Jesus nicknamed him "Rocky," but he was anything but a Rock. He was more like sand.

What mission does God have in mind for you? He knows what it is although you might not look like a likely candidate for it. Anyone can count the apples on a tree, but only a person of faith can count the trees in an apple. Jesus sees much more in you than you do. He wants to do His mission through you like He did with Peter.

Peter next encountered the Savior in Capernaum. We don't know what happened between the time of Peter's first meeting with Jesus in Judea and this one. God was always at work around Peter just as He is at work around you.

Reality #2: God pursues a continuing love relationship with Peter and you that is real and personal. We next meet Peter when Jesus went to Peter's home (Luke 4:38–44). Jesus healed Peter's mother-in-law of a high fever and then healed others. Because He loves us, Jesus keeps pursuing us into our homes and with our families.

Reality #3: God invites you to become involved with Him in His work. Later as Jesus taught the crowds by the Lake of Gennesaret (Luke 5:1–11), He was so mobbed by people that He looked around and found a couple of fishing boats. Picking Simon's boat was no accident. Jesus involved him in His mission! I wonder how Peter felt about that since he was tired of fishing all night. Jesus got in the boat with Peter and taught the multitude while Peter with no way to escape eavesdropped from the other end of the boat.

God wants to get into your boat. He is at work where you work. Whether or not you recognize or expect it, He has a plan and a purpose for you. Are you aware of what He is doing where you work? Has He invited you to work with Him there?

Reality #4: God speaks to you personally. When Jesus finished addressing the multitude, He zeroed in on Peter. He said, "Put out into deep water, and let down the nets for a catch" (Luke 5:4). Peter respectfully addressed him as "Master" but proceeded to give him the experienced fisherman's point of view! Peter was probably tired and discouraged after working hard all night and not catching anything. But when he heard the voice of God, he obeyed.

Daily you face that choice: to hear or not hear. You may think you know what your job is—even in kingdom work—and may consider yourself an expert at what you do. Like Peter, you may have toiled diligently at a project, only to be discouraged. In such times, avoid citing reasons for your failure and listen for God's voice.

Reality #5: God's invitation to be on mission for Him will lead you to a crisis of belief that requires faith and action. Peter protested, "Master, we've worked hard all night and haven't caught anything" (v. 5). What would you expect Peter to say next? Surprisingly, he said, "But because you say so, I will let down the nets."

God is in the business of saying what He will do in the future. God speaks to His servants, and what you do next shows how much you believe God. Peter obeyed because he believed! In my own experience, at every critical point in my life, God has led me by a Word from Him. Often I wasn't ready to receive that word.

163

Sometimes it was a difficult word. At other times it was such a good word that I couldn't imagine it could happen. But God speaks through His Word and waits for us to obey.

When Peter obeyed he and his friends caught so many fish that their newly mended nets began to break. They called their partners, "Come and help us!" When you believe and act on what God tells you to do, He will surprise you. Stop now and ask God to show you what He wants you to believe He will do in your life (Eph. 3:20).

Reality #6: You must make major adjustments in your life to join God in what He is doing. When Peter realized what Jesus had done, he cried, "Go away from me, Lord; I am a sinful man!" Why did he say he was sinful? I think he said it because he hadn't really believed Jesus. Peter repented and admitted his sin. Jesus went a step further and added a challenge to his comforting words, "Don't be afraid; from now on you will catch men." Now that introduced a crisis of belief in this fisherman's life that would involve a major adjustment!

God gets involved in your work, to get you involved in His work. You may interpret God's action in your life as merely a special blessing for you when God intends for it to become a crisis of belief that propels you into His mission.

Reality #7: You experience God's glory as you obey Him and He accomplishes His work through you. You not only see proof of Peter's life-changing encounter with Jesus in the words he spoke but also in his actions. He could have just gone home after this experience, told his wife and mother-in-law what a great time he had had with Jesus, and settled down to his daily routine.

But faith without obedience is dead. The Lord got through to Peter by a living analogy that he understood. Jesus promised that Peter would catch many men, just as he had caught fish (Luke 5:11). This was a costly decision, but Peter and his companions were willing to leave their boats on the shore to experience an intimate relationship with Christ.

We have looked at the earliest episodes in the life of Peter's experience with Jesus. Jesus changed his name from Simon to Cephas (the Aramaic term for *rock*). Later, Jesus referred to him as Peter (the Greek term for *rock*). At that point Peter was anything but a rock. Mercury, maybe—but a rock? No. Jesus knew what He had chosen Peter to be and with this nickname gave him a hint of his mission with God. These first experiences with Jesus and Peter's obedience launched his ship into the middle of a river of experiences with God.

PETER'S WIDE-ANGLE VIEW OF A LIFETIME OF EXPERIENCING GOD

Let's look at how the Seven Spiritual Markers played out in the life of Peter. By now you should be feeling comfortable with viewing your life from these seven vantage points. However, each character presents the potential of a new view of yourself in relationship to them.

Spiritual Marker #1: God chooses you. God chose Peter even though he had numerous faults—perhaps the worst being impulsiveness. Without thinking, he tended to blurt out whatever first came to his mind. This often got him into trouble. Even after following Jesus for a year and a half and uttering God-revealed, earth-shaking revelations, he messed up (Matt. 16:13–23). At one moment He was a mouthpiece for God; the next, He spoke the words of Satan. Imagine a human being rebuking the Son of God! He was so proud of the revelation that God had just given him that he thought he knew everything. Have you ever done the same thing? Even knowing the mistakes you would make, God chose you.

Spiritual Marker #2: God calls you to Himself to be on mission with Him. Peter's call was very clear. He was one of the first whom Jesus called to be a disciple (Mark 1:16–20). Later, he would be called out and commissioned as an apostle (Mark 3:13–19). Peter's name is at the head of every list of the twelve that Jesus called to be on mission with Him!

In the first call Jesus walked beside the Sea of Galilee and in the second He called Peter and the others from a mountain. The first calling was to four disciples, but the second included all twelve apostles. The first time, they left their nets to follow Him, and the second, to attach themselves to Him. The first time they left their occupation, and the second time they took up His mission. Note that Jesus called all of His disciples and apostles first to be with Him. Their intimate relationship with the Son of God would be the wellspring out of which their ministry flowed to bless others. That was the key to their being on mission with Him as they were sent out as apostles to preach with His authority.

Today God calls us to Himself, so that we can walk intimately with Him and work passionately for Him. In time He will send you to do what is on His heart. Your mission may be in your neighborhood or in the inner city. It may involve leaving your occupation or your relatives behind. Whatever He asks you to do will result in your being appointed and anointed to join Him on an exciting kingdom mission that will result in your experiencing God's glory!

Spiritual Marker #3: God initiates a covenant of promise and obedience with you. The Lord made a covenant with Peter, even as He made a covenant with Abraham and Moses. He effectively said, "Follow me, and I will make you a fisher of men. I promise you, Peter, it's going to be better than what you just saw when the nets were breaking. You will fish for men." Jesus saw the day when Peter would cast the net with one sermon and see three thousand people come into the kingdom! Peter couldn't see that yet.

What does God have in mind for you that you haven't yet believed? You may say, "I'm sinful, God; you know that. I don't have great faith. I can't do things that some other folks do." Peter was like that. But Jesus promises, "You follow me, and I'm going to make you a fisher of men." That word of promise from God demands obedience.

The first word I remember God giving me that I claimed as His promise to me was Matthew 6:33. The second word He gave me was Psalm 71:17–18, and it was even more of a challenge to me. I agreed that from my youth I had declared His marvelous deeds. I could not imagine what it meant for me "to declare His power to the next generation and His might to all who will come" (NASB). For twenty-five years I didn't share that promise with anyone because it sounded both presumptuous and frightening. However, I said, "God, I really believe You have given me this promise because the Holy Spirit has impressed it on my heart. I'm going to apply this verse to my life and watch to see what You do."

167

Forty years later I am beginning to see how God is fulfilling His promise to me through my writing *MasterLife* and other books, my ministry in Indonesia and America, and now around the world as I oversee the overseas strategy and work of the International Mission Board. Again and again God has lifted me, as it were, by my bootstraps, reminding me of this promise or challenging me with a Word that said, "This is what I am going to do through you, an ordinary person, so I will get the glory."

You need a vision for your life. I'm not talking about visioning in the sense that business does. To business leaders that word means "dream as big as you can and go for it." Not on your life! Peter discovered visions from God involve three things:

1. Life visions must be God revealed, not humanly conceived. If you thought it up, it probably isn't from God. Through His Word, prayer, circumstances, and other Christians' counsel, God will help you understand His vision for your life. He may not tell you everything now, but He will give you enough insight for you to respond with the next step.

2. Life visions from God are so big you cannot accomplish them yourself. If you can accomplish them yourself, then they are probably not from God. God gives visions that make you depend on Him and involve other people for their accomplishment so He will get the glory.

3. Life visions that come from God are life arrangers. When your priorities are arranged correctly, many other decisions become easier. As a Christian youth I remember committing, "God, I want to keep myself pure for my future wife." My best friend responded, "That sounds stupid." But that commitment helped me say no when faced with tough decisions. Because I

made the big commitment, other decisions became easier. When you make the right commitments to accomplish your vision, it helps you narrow your focus to concentrate on what God really wants to do in your life.

God will give you a vision also. In fact, He probably already has. Are you aware of it and that it came from Him? Be alert for a life vision from God as you read His Word.

Spiritual Marker #4: God prepares you for His mission. Peter needed the Lord to prepare Him for an entirely new mission in life. From fearful fisherman to fearless apostle was a long stretch for Peter. God knows how much preparation is required in your life to get you to the point where you are equipped to be an effective colaborer with Him. The three years of preparation must have seemed like thirty to Peter. When you first commit to God's call, you think, *I'm going out and win the world.* Many young preachers have had someone tell them, "You'll be another Billy Graham." But God has to take them through a lot to develop their character to match their assignments.

Have you ever stopped to count how many years God has been preparing you for your mission? Don't be concerned if it seems like a long time. Just remember the time lines of preparation for the seven mentors you are studying. God takes time to build the character into you that will make you what He is calling you to be. In this case, Peter was called "a rock." But Jesus had to add a lot of concrete to the sand to make Peter a rock. God mixed tough times in with the good times to accomplish His will in Peter's life. Often you become more like God during the tough times than you do during the good times. He prepares you to make right choices and live according to His values. Be aware that in difficult experiences God is developing your character for His mission.

Christ took many corrective measures as He walked with Peter. After the resurrection, one major event changed Peter's life and the lives of the other apostles forever—the coming of the Holy Spirit at Pentecost. Something dramatic happened to Peter between the last chapter of John and the first chapter of Acts. After Christ gave the Great Commission and ascended to heaven, Peter joined 120 of Jesus' followers obediently waiting in the upper room.

During ten days of prayer, God rearranged their thinking as they waited for the Holy Spirit to come. Look how He prepared them. First, He grounded them in the Word (Luke 24:44–49; Acts 1:15–22). Peter began to lead. Using the Scriptures, he led those present to replace Judas on the apostolic team. Before Pentecost the disciples never quoted Scripture. After Pentecost they quoted Scripture in every message. Second, God prepared their hearts through prayer! As they prayed, God brought them to a great unity. Third, God prepared them to wait expectantly in faith for the Holy Spirit to empower them for the work they were to do.

What was to happen in the church had to happen first to Peter. The Lord wants to empower His church. To do that He empowers its members as individuals. Do you embody what God wants to do with the people with whom you are associated—your family, your church, and your ministry team? Is your prayer, "Oh, God, make me the person you want me to be so You can accomplish what You want in my church through my life?"

Suddenly it happened—not only to Peter but also to all the apostles at Pentecost. They were all filled with the Holy Spirit.

They would never be the same again. Peter was transformed from fearful to fearless, from faithless to faithful. Have you been filled, and are you daily being filled with the Spirit for the task to which He has called you? (Luke 24:44–49; Eph. 5:18). Ask God to fill you and empower you for the work He has called you to do.

Spiritual Marker #5: God sends you to the place where He can best work through you to accomplish His mission. Peter had the privilege of being at the hub of things with Jesus—one of three in His inner circle, along with James and John. The trio represented the only ones allowed to experience several life-changing situations. Chief among these were the raising of the young daughter of Jairus from the dead (Mark 5:37–43; Luke 8:51–56), Christ's transfiguration (Matt. 17:1–2), and being asked to pray during the Lord's agony in Gethsemane (Matt. 26:37–45; Mark 14:33–41). Through these events, the Lord wanted these three to experience His power, His glory, and His prayer life at close range so they would remember these extraordinary events after He appointed them to lead the early church. Peter was also trained along with the other disciples through the special missions Christ sent them on during His earthly ministry.

Have you ever felt you have failed the Lord so badly that He will never send you on another mission? Even then, God does not give up on you. Peter fell terribly far when he denied his Lord three times. After that, Peter must have felt that any ministry for him was over. But the Lord had not given up on Peter. He allowed him to be the first disciple to witness His resurrection from the dead (Luke 24:34; 1 Cor. 15:5). Later, when He met with Peter at the Sea of Galilee, He challenged him to affirm his love for Him three times to counter those three dreadful denials. Peter wasn't finished at all. Instead, Jesus wanted to send a humbled, repentant Peter to feed His sheep.

Note the interesting similarities between Peter's initial call to follow Christ and this postresurrection encounter with the risen Lord. Jesus seems to want to give Peter a fresh start in all the areas where he had failed to live up to his "rock" potential. Today, if you sense that you have failed the Lord, He wants to restore you to full fellowship with Himself. Then He can send you, like Peter, on a new assignment—to feed His lambs and tend His sheep and not just to catch fish.

Spiritual Marker #6: God guides you on your mission with Him. For three years Peter knew the one-on-one personal guidance from Jesus (2 Pet. 1:16–18). After Christ's ascension, Peter enjoyed the glory of the Holy Spirit's personal presence and guidance under trying circumstances. What an incredible experience that must have been for Peter to experience God's glory in the personal guidance of these two members of the Godhead under the Father's direction!

In a fascinating incident of God's guidance, Peter obviously was trying to figure out what the Lord wanted him to do when faced by a crippled beggar (Acts 3:1–10). As he looked intently at the crippled man, the Holy Spirit guided him to take the next step. Peter commanded him in Jesus' name to walk! He was also led to take him by the right hand and help him to his feet. When an astonished crowd gathered around, Peter realized that the Lord had given him a perfect platform for preaching the gospel. The next day, after spending the night in jail for this act of mercy, Peter was filled with the Holy Spirit and spoke powerful words before the rulers, elders, and teachers of the law.

Have you ever been in a spot like Peter was? If so, you will appreciate how helpless he would have felt without the Lord's guidance. He had experienced his own limitations and now depended totally on God for His guidance and power. He became a transformed person and allowed the Lord to work through him.

Spiritual Marker #7: God uses you to bring glory to His name through His mission. Everyone remembers Peter's failures, but in history, he is known for his role at Pentecost and for leading the first church. Through his example and his writings, Peter's life still casts a shadow today (Acts 5:15). Have you ever thought about what kind of "spiritual will" you would like to leave as a legacy? You cannot start a spiritual awakening, nor can you start a church-planting movement. Neither could Peter, but God used him to do both. God has a purpose for your life among His people, and you are writing a legacy whether you realize it or not.

PETER'S 180-DEGREE VIEW OF GOD DEVELOPING A CHURCH FOR ALL PEOPLE

What a makeover God did in Peter's life! Meeting him before and after Pentecost, you would not believe he was the same person. God had more in mind than just changing Peter. He intended to launch a church for all peoples. He chose Peter to be the leader through whom He would work. Jesus knew strong leadership was required to launch a church for all peoples. That's why He spent so much time discipling Peter and the other apostles. Christ wanted a firm foundation for His church as it faced a hostile, pagan world. Look now at how God used the Seven Spiritual Markers with His whole people to get them on mission with Him.

Corporate Spiritual Marker #1: God chose His people to be a church on mission with Him. If you were choosing church leadership for today, you would probably be tempted to choose people with the best personalities, abilities, and gifting. You would probably also choose people who are well-educated, influential, wise, physically attractive, and wealthy. We are naturally attracted to people like that. But the group Jesus chose lacked in most of those areas. They were weak, lowly, and despised (1 Cor. 1:26–31).

James and John were called "Sons of Thunder." Matthew was a hated publican who collaborated with the Roman government. Simon, "the Zealot," was a revolutionary trying to overthrow the Romans. "Doubting" Thomas was an unlikely overcomer, as were most of the disciples whom we know only by name. Peter, the usual leader, seemed to have some of the worst warts! But each disciple was chosen to fulfill the Father's purpose.

If you believe you are foolish, weak, lowly, and despised, you are exactly what the Lord is looking for. God can use you and other "misfits" to disable the mighty empires of this modern age. He has done it ever since confounding the Jews and Romans in the first century. Even if you and others in your church are highly educated, wealthy, wise, and respected, recognize that without God's working in you, you can do nothing of eternal value. He looks for a humble group of people to join Him on mission! That's why He chose your church and is working with you.

Corporate Spiritual Marker #2: God calls His people to establish a church for all peoples. Have you ever considered that you might be called to lead in Christ's church, as Peter was? You might reply, "No way!" I'm sure Peter was surprised at the great changes the Lord made in his life and the catalyst he would become in the body of Christ. Through Peter's weaknesses God demonstrated how the Holy Spirit empowers His people to be His witnesses to all peoples.

As you experience God on mission, you will be amazed at His aims for you, the shame you will feel at your failures, the fact that He will reclaim you and that people may even acclaim you as a leader. But that is how God works among His people to impact the world. Empowered by the Holy Spirit, Peter was fearless and courageous before the authorities. Above all, that is what the world needs to know. Have you been with Jesus? (see Acts 4:13). The educated elite of that day took note that Peter and John had been with Jesus!

God's purpose is to use all of His people—not just some of His people or just His leaders. God wants to use you and your church as He used Peter and the first church, as world-changing catalysts. You are called to stand before the world's authorities and witness boldly about Christ. He calls all His people, even those with great weaknesses, to be on mission with Him!

Think about how God could use you as a catalyst to move your church toward spiritual awakening and to being on mission with God. Have you ever thought about being part of a round-the-clock prayer chain to pray for revival? Or have you ever considered finding a prayer partner and committing to praying for your church's renewal or studying revivals in God's Word and sharing the burden with others, or prayerwalking your church building, praying that revival will occur there?

Two women in London, England, who prayed for many years were credited by many as the cause of the revival during D. L. Moody's crusades there. Every great revival has been preceded by obscure praying people who have a heart for God and His mission. God may call you to be the person He uses to awaken His church to its mission.

Corporate Spiritual Marker #3: God initiates a covenant of promise and obedience with His church. Throughout the Bible, God reaches out to His people by forming covenants with them. Among the more famous is the covenant in 2 Chronicles 7:14: "If my people, who are called by my name, will humble themselves and pray and seek my face and turn from their wicked ways, then will I hear from heaven and will forgive their sin and will heal their land." Note that the key words in this covenant as well as in others are "if" and "then." God says in effect, "If you will do this, then I will do that."

If God told the people in your church to stop everything and spend ten days in prayer for revival, how would they respond? God promises you power if you wait on Him. One reason for powerlessness today is the fact that the secular crowds out the spiritual.

Jesus fed five thousand people; five hundred saw Him at one time after His resurrection, but only 120 took His promise seriously and waited and prayed in the upper room until the Holy Spirit came on them. What percentage of the people in your church do you think are waiting for the Holy Spirit's empowering today? (Luke 24:49). Does your answer surprise you?

Jesus invites you to be a part of His empowered body to go on mission with Him. Along with that, He promises to be with you to the end of the age. Revival will come to you personally and to your church when you become an Acts 1:8 church, abandon your personal agendas for kingdom purposes, and wait on God to fill you to overflowing with His Spirit. Among the signs of an empowered body are powerful prayer meetings. Become part of a prayer group in your church that is having a significant impact even if you have to start one or are the only one.

Corporate Spiritual Marker #4: God prepares His church for His mission in the world. God prepared His people at Pentecost through corporate prayer. Nothing makes you more transparent with the Lord than does praying with others. One reason God had the 120 together in the upper room for ten days before the Holy Spirit came on them was to unify them. He knew they needed to bond to prepare to handle the influx of three thousand people who would soon come into the church.

We can say, "God, do again among your people what you did in Acts." But it will take a unifying and empowering move of the Spirit among us.

You may say, "I or my church certainly couldn't be used to bring spiritual awakening." But in the history of spiritual awakenings, God chose the people you would least expect to be catalysts for revival. When God speaks to you and your church, don't say no but "Yes, Lord, your servants hear." God has a unique mission for every church. Discover what it is. Then help your church get in position for God to use it.

Corporate Spiritual Marker #5: God sends His church on mission where He can best work through them to accomplish His mission. God sometimes takes drastic measures to get His people to go where He has already told them to go but they have been unwilling to go. About ten years after Pentecost, the disciples were still in Jerusalem. God used persecution to send His people on mission (Acts 8:4). The apostles stayed in Jerusalem, but the Lord worked so powerfully through Philip in Samaria that the church in Jerusalem sent Peter and John to help them out! (Acts 8:1–24).

The members of the early church were scattered abroad by persecution, taking the gospel with them and declaring it with great boldness. In the first century, a supportive synergy occurred in their working together to reach beyond their home church.

In Acts, spiritual awakening occurred among ordinary people. One of the greatest needs in America and throughout Christianity is a spiritual awakening that will lead to church-planting movements among the unreached peoples of the world. Encourage your church to seek after God so that He can use you to do what only He can do among the people to whom He sends you.

Corporate Spiritual Marker #6: God guides His church when they are on mission. Have you ever been in such a confusing situation that you needed God's instant guidance to discern exactly what was happening? That happened to Peter when he went to Samaria to help with the revival there. Simon the sorcerer, known there as "the Great Power" because of his magic, put Peter's reliance on God's guidance to the test (Acts 8:9–24).

Simon the Magician put on a good show before the apostles came to Samaria. He might have gone on fooling everyone if Peter had not relied on God for guidance. God has placed the church of Jesus in confusing and evil times. The body of Christ needs to have such an intimate relationship with the Lord that it can discern immediately who and what is of God. Otherwise, great damage will be done to the cause of Christ (2 Tim. 3:1–5).

The Holy Spirit's guidance is what makes the difference. You will know where He wants you to go, what He wants you to say, and what He wants you to do as you join Him on mission (1 Cor. 2:14–15).

Corporate Spiritual Marker #7: God uses His corporate people to fulfill His mission. God mightily used Peter, first as he went throughout Judea and Samaria, and later as he went to the sea-coast towns. God used him to heal a paralytic and raise a woman from the dead! No doubt Peter thought he was right on track, but he had forgotten the rest of the story in Acts 1:8.

THE 360-DEGREE ETERNAL PERSPECTIVE OF HOW GOD USED PETER TO DEVELOP A CHURCH FOR ALL PEOPLES

God fulfills His eternal purpose through His people as they obey Him. Take a few moments and read Acts 10, and then we will talk about how this experience became a pivotal point in God's eternal mission.

Approximately ten years had passed since Christ gave the Great Commission. At Pentecost people of many languages and nations had heard the "amazing works of God," but that did not seem to impact the disciples with the urgency of being Christ's witness equally in Jerusalem, Judea, Samaria, and the ends of the earth. Peter and the church still concentrated on the Jews. Many sheep from other folds needed to hear the gospel.

A few miracles that brought God glory were not sufficient when Christ's commission was still waiting to be carried out. God had planned for all peoples to glorify Him. He would use Peter as the pivotal point to set the church free to do what it was designed to do. Peter would be that rock that would be the launching pad for the church on mission. God still had to do in Peter's life what

He planned to do in the church. He had to set him on fire so the church would go beyond anything they had ever envisioned! Through them God communicated the eternal message that God gave the church through Peter.

Evaluate the percentage of prayer, going, and giving that your church does in each of these four assignments: Jerusalem—the place where it is located, Judea—the area surrounding you, Samaria—the area beyond your kind of people, and in the ends of the earth—the rest of the world. Look how God revealed His will for all people through Peter's experience.

Eternal Truth #1: God initiates conviction in the hearts of the lost out beyond the church. Only a few miles away from where Peter was ministering in Joppa, Cornelius sought God, but he didn't know how to be saved. God sent a vision in which Cornelius saw and heard an angel speak to him. The angel didn't tell him how to be saved but directed him to send men to Joppa to ask for Peter. Angels can't witness about salvation because they have never experienced lostness or salvation. That's why God uses saved sinners—people He has redeemed—to tell the story.

Today God works among all peoples, causing many to seek Him. In a country where a Christian witness is restricted, a man arrived at the house of a Christian representative from America. The Christian asked, "Can I help you?" He said, "I have had a vision for the last three years on the last night of the forty-day fast, Ramadan. As you know, we Muslims believe that God gives revelations on the last night of the fast just before the holy day, Idul Fitri. For the last three years on that night I have dreamed of Jesus coming to me and saying, 'Follow me.' Last night I had that same dream again. This time He said, 'Follow me.' Then He added, 'Go to the house of the foreigner. He will tell you how to follow Me.' Can you tell me how to follow Him?" God still takes the initiative among the thousands of Muslims who report seeing Jesus in dreams and hearing Him beckon them to follow Him.

I met a Hindu man in Myanmar (formerly Burma) who also dreamed of Jesus. In the dream Jesus told him to go to another village and talk to a friend of his who would tell him about the Book. When he did, the friend said, "The man in your dream is Jesus. The Book is the Bible. I am not a Christian myself, but I know one in another village. He has the Book. Go ask him." When the man arrived at the other village, the Christian explained how he could be saved. The Hindu man believed. In a few weeks he had led twenty-six persons to Christ. The Hindu village forced him to leave. He went to his wife's village, twenty kilometers away, and soon won twenty-three people there. I met them the week they were baptized in Yangoon.

God is at work all over the world in unusual ways convicting people that they need a Savior. But like God's people in Peter's day, many are not listening to Him when He sends them to the lost. Some even have prejudices or beliefs that keep them from witnessing to others who differ from them. Peter couldn't imagine Gentiles (another word for all peoples) following Christ, although throughout Scripture, God has revealed that He is concerned for all people.

Eternal Truth #2: God interrupts His people to involve them in His mission. Meanwhile God was at work in Joppa to get Peter ready to go tell Cornelius how to be saved. God came to Cornelius in a vision, but He put Peter in a trance before Peter could hear him. The Lord started the encounter with Cornelius before He shocked Peter into seeing what He was doing. The key component in both cases was prayer. God was at work in both places at the same time to bring about a breakthrough that Peter could never have imagined. He was too prejudiced to hear God on this issue!

Many Christian cultures are bound on the north, south, east, and west by themselves and people like them. Strangers and people of different races are overlooked. God wants to raise the sights of His church to catch a glimpse of His global vision.

In the midst of all Peter's good works, God interrupted him to teach him God's heart for all peoples. While Peter waited on the rooftop, praying, he fell into a trance. He saw something that looked like a sheet coming from heaven with all kinds of animals, reptiles, and birds that were unclean, according to the Old Testament laws and Jewish tradition. He heard God say, "Get up, Peter. Kill and eat" (Acts 10:13 NIV). Peter couldn't believe his ears. Yet it clearly was the voice of God. He had heard God's voice at Jesus' baptism and on the Mount of Transfiguration, so he recognized it. Peter could have responded by saying, "Yes, Lord, yes!" Instead he said, "Surely not, Lord! I have never eaten anything impure or unclean" (v. 14). He couldn't imagine God commanding him to do this.

Has God told you to do something that goes against your church's traditions or is outside your normal experience, and you protested that He couldn't possibly mean what you heard Him say? Jesus said that His sheep hear His voice. Instead of acting like an obedient sheep, Peter returned to his billy goat days of "but, but, but . . . ."

Three times the Lord insisted, "Get up, Peter. Kill and eat" (v. 16). It usually took three times to get through to Peter. Peter denied the Lord three times. Jesus asked Peter three times after the resurrection, "Peter, do you love me?" Now He told Peter three times, "Get up, Peter. Kill and eat."

The Lord stayed right in Peter's face by continuing to drop the sheet full of unclean animals in front of him. This experience was totally opposite to anything Peter had ever seen or believed. Talk about tradition getting in the way! Peter didn't just have tradition; he had the whole Old Testament to back him up! He might have said, "Lord, I can show you chapter and verse." Understandably Peter was confused. His theology did not match what God was saying. God will interrupt your traditions to get you to follow His commands that you have neglected to obey.

Every step of growth or more effective ministry that God has initiated in my life has felt like an interruption, at least in its timing. God interrupted me to save me. He interrupted me in my apathetic Christian life to move me into becoming a true disciple. He interrupted my comfortable life to call me to be a missionary. Against my personal desires He led me to move from being a frontline missionary to teach at and later lead a seminary. When I did not respond immediately, He let circumstances occur that demanded that I listen to Him. When I thought I would be a missionary for life, He shocked me by calling me back to the United States to disciple others to be on mission. In fact, the only major move that He has initiated in my life that has not felt like an interruption has been to my present role. Maybe, at last, I've learned to obey without arguing about what God wanted me to do!

You may say, "I'm doing a lot of good. God uses me where I am." That's what Peter, the recognized Christian leader of his day, thought! When God interrupts you, don't reply as Peter did, "No, Lord." In fact, "No, Lord," is an oxymoron. If He is Lord, you can't say no. If you say no, He isn't Lord in your life.

Eternal Truth #3: God instructs the committed as they go on mission with Him. While Peter was still trying to understand the meaning of abandoning his traditions, the Holy Spirit timed His further instructions perfectly: "Simon, three men are looking for you. So get up and go downstairs. Do not hesitate to go with them, for I have sent them" (vv. 19–20 NIV). Peter surely would have hesitated to go with them if the Spirit had not been so specific! How did God lead Peter to obey in the face of all his tradition? The Holy Spirit spoke first through prayer, then through the living Word of God, and finally through circumstances. Before the story ends, the Spirit leads Peter and the church to declare the mystery of God that had been hidden for ages—that all peoples are to worship and serve Him.

Do you ever feel like Peter after the trance? Are you confused? Do things not add up? While Peter pondered these strange things, God engineered the next step in the saga. He still didn't know what God was up to, but God instructed him clearly by saying, "Simon, three men are at the gate. Go with them, doubting nothing, for I have sent them."

Peter responded immediately. He invited the men to stay overnight. However, he took his time getting from Joppa to Caesarea. In fact, he took three times as long to make the trip as the men had taken to come to him. At least he wasn't like the prophet Jonah, who centuries before headed in the opposite direction from Joppa!

Although he did not know what God was leading him to do, Peter followed. You, too, may have sensed God speaking to you as you have read the experiences of these biblical characters. If you obey Him God will give you more light. For instance, a flashlight will shine perhaps fifty feet or fifty yards, depending on how bright the beam is. But it won't shine one bit farther until you take a step toward the light. Every step you take toward the light, the farther the light shines.

God instructed Peter on the way when Peter got out of the way. However, this was not easy. When he got to Cornelius's house, he was offensive at first. He said, "You are well aware that it is against our law for a Jew to associate with a Gentile or visit him" (Acts 10:28 NIV). Obviously Peter had not read *How to Win Friends and Influence People!* Cornelius, however, graciously replied, "It was good of you to come. My family and friends have been waiting four days for you."

Peter went on to say, "But God has shown me that I should not call any man impure or unclean" (v. 28 NIV). At least he had correctly interpreted the vision and didn't talk about bedsheet smorgasbords. "So when I was sent for, I came without raising any objection." That was half true. When the men arrived, he did not object to them, but he had objected plenty to God! Peter began to understand the vision: "I now realize how true it is that God does not show favoritism but accepts men from every nation who fear him and do what is right" (vv. 34–35 NIV). God instructs you along the way, as He did Peter. I am glad God did not show all He had in mind when He first interrupted me. I might have backed out. When the time arrived, He revealed His will, providing the resources I needed.

Eternal Truth #4: God intervenes to complete His plan as you and His church obey Him. Peter may not have been too happy with his assignment at first, but God's heart must have thrilled to see His kingdom established in the hearts of the Gentiles. God's grand design was coming to fruition. In fact, God couldn't wait for Peter to finish his sermon. He interrupted him right in the middle of it! "While Peter was still speaking these words, the Holy Spirit came down on all those who heard the message. The circumcised believers who had come with Peter were astounded because the gift of the Holy Spirit had been poured out on the Gentiles also" (Acts 10:44–45).

Perhaps you and your church are like Peter and the first church, wondering what God is doing with you and saying to you. But when you hear the voice of God, just respond to Him. If the Lord says some things that don't make sense to you, stay before Him. Wait on Him. Do what He says. When you follow Him, God will bless you and bless others through you.

Because Peter obeyed and delivered the message God desired, the Holy Spirit came on all who heard the message. Everyone believed and was baptized in the Holy Spirit and in water. Almost one-third of the people in the world still wait to hear the first word of the gospel. I believe that millions of them would believe any day of the week if the gospel were just explained to them in a way they could understand culturally. Another third have potentially heard the gospel but have not understood it, so they have not believed. Another third have the gospel but have not shared it. People throughout the world wait for us to share the message with them so that God may be glorified among all peoples!

Be aware in your own heart of any prejudice toward others that keeps you or your church from fully accepting them and witnessing to them. Ask God to rid you of that prejudice. And also be cognizant of certain peoples whom God has sensitized your heart toward. That sensitivity, I believe, is an indication of God at work in your life.

Eternal Truth #5: God intends to use His church until He is glorified by all peoples. Have you ever done what you believed God told you to do and gotten into trouble for doing it? Peter was usually in trouble, so it probably didn't surprise him that he was criticized for preaching the gospel to the Gentiles! Some of the first church's leaders were absolutely convinced that Peter didn't do right. Things haven't changed much, have they? (Acts 11:1–18).

Peter was wise in taking six circumcised Jewish believers with him when he went to Cornelius's house. When he returned to Jerusalem, he took with him all six to establish the truth of his testimony. He also answered wisely, because he told his critics exactly what happened. He gave a report to this effect: "I didn't finish my sermon. I didn't give an invitation. I had just started preaching." (It will take you less than five minutes to read what he preached in Acts 10:34–43.) "When I got to the place where all the prophets bear witness that this Jesus is the Son of God and that through His name forgiveness of sin is given—wow! They believed, just like that. God interrupted my sermon to send the baptism in the Holy Spirit on them just as He had on us. Who was I to oppose God?" Pretty good answer, don't you think? He depended totally on God to give him the right words in this delicate situation.

The good news is, "When they heard this, they had no further objections and praised God, saying, 'So then, God has granted even the Gentiles repentance unto life'" (Acts 11:18 NIV). You can almost hear the incredulity in their voices! Their borders had been enlarged; they had no choice but to go to the ends of the earth to reach all those Gentiles! They knew the Great Commission, but it took an experience with God to motivate them to fulfill it.

The eternal truth of Peter's life was that the Holy Spirit worked through him to empower the church and send them out to reach all peoples!

God has a plan for your life as He did for Peter's life. Peter's kind of obedience is necessary to hear God, to know what He wants, to be available to be used by God to do what He wants to do in your life. Only through God's people will the unreached be reached. Nothing else will satisfy God or bring Him the glory He deserves!

7

PAUL ON MISSION WITH GOD

THE GOSPEL FOR ALL PEOPLES

"For God, who said, 'Light shall shine out of
darkness'—He has shone in our hearts to give the light
of the knowledge of God's glory in the face of Jesus
Christ. Now we have this treasure in clay jars, so that
this extraordinary power may be from God and not
from us."

—2 Corinthians 4:6–7

I TALKED TO SOME MISSIONARIES IN A RESISTANT AFRICAN COUNTRY
who were studying *Experiencing God* together. They had experienced little positive results. They felt that somehow they weren't
applying what they were learning. They went on a prayer retreat
in a government park to ask God where He was working.

Early one morning, one of the single women exercised by walking down the road near the park. A young man walking up the

189

road stopped her and asked why she was in that part of Africa. She told him her group were Christians and were there to pray. The Muslim young man was surprised because he didn't think Christians prayed much. As he asked more questions, she realized that he was seeking God. She took him back to camp, where a friend who knew his heart language, Zarma, shared Christ with him. He trusted Christ on the spot. He asked them to go out to his village in the bush and tell his family. The woman who led him to Christ along with a missionary couple went with the young man seventeen kilometers into the bush, all the time wondering if their Land Rover would get hijacked in the process! They told the village chief that at the young man's request they had come to tell his family about Jesus. The chief asked, "Why should they hear it and not all the rest of us hear it?" He invited the whole village to come together at the afternoon siesta time. The man preached while his colleague translated. He told about the first African who came to know Christ—the Ethiopian eunuch. In the middle of the gospel story, the Muslim call to prayer occurred. Some got up and washed, said prayers, and returned for the rest of the story. At the end the missionary issued an invitation.

An elderly man came forward and drew two lines in the sand. He said, "There must be two ways to God." The missionary said the one verse he had memorized in Zarma: "Jesus said, I am the way, the truth and light. No man comes to the Father but by Me." With that, the old man said, "I thought so. Jesus' way must be the way. How do we do it?" It took about twenty or thirty minutes to teach them how to pray to receive Christ. Then fourteen men stood up, shoulder to shoulder, and professed faith in Christ right there.

Later, when the missionaries went back to check on them, they said, "We've already been over to the next village and told them and another person believed. So we discipled and baptized him. Is that OK?" From the simple request of God about where He was working has sprung an incredible harvest of souls in a restricted country that continues today!

Paul did not start out as a missionary. In fact, before he met Jesus, Paul was not a likable fellow. According to whom? Christians or Sanhedrin? His major weakness was his confidence in what he could do. Incredibly zealous, he persecuted the church of God. The Sanhedrin likely said, "Go to it, Saul. We gave you the best education we could give you under Gamaliel. Go stop those Christians!" Like powerful religious leaders often do, they got him to do their dirty work. Like zealous young people in every age, Saul did. But while he was headed the wrong way, Saul was about to experience God!

PAUL'S CLOSE-UP VIEW OF EXPERIENCING GOD

Reality #1: God is at work around you even when you are working against Him. God was at work all around Saul of Tarsus, but Saul missed Him completely. He was so focused on what he would do for God that he missed what God was doing. He didn't see that God was using everything that happened to the young churches to accomplish His purpose. Somehow God began to penetrate his heart. It may have started when Gamaliel gave to the Sanhedrin the advice recorded in Acts 5:38–39.

The experience that most piqued Saul's conscience was the stoning of Stephen. As Saul raged toward Damascus, he couldn't forget how Stephen died while he held the clothes of those who killed him. Perhaps he could still hear Stephen saying, "Lord, do not hold this sin against them" (Acts 7:60 NIV). Suddenly Jesus appeared to him in a blinding light and said, "Saul, Saul, why are you persecuting Me? It is hard for you to kick against the goads"(Acts 26:14). Goads were sharpened sticks protruding out of a cart to keep the oxen from kicking. Saul kicked one too many times. Persecution and martyrdom are fertilizer for the church. Most church-planting movements don't occur without suffering.

Godly men buried Stephen, and the apostles stayed in Jerusalem. However, because of the persecution that arose after Stephen's death, the disciples were scattered and went everywhere preaching. Saul went after them, wreaking havoc among God's people. His zeal drove him to imprison men and women. But God did not permit Saul to pursue "righteousness" in his own rebellious fashion; He brought Saul to a screeching halt! The Lord met him face-to-face on the road to Damascus. This unexpected event—a life-changing encounter with the risen Lord—changed Saul forever.

In every movement of God, you'll find people who fought God and Christianity with all their might, only to be conquered by Christ and become His zealous disciples. Even when you work against God, God works all around you. Any time you see someone opposing God, remember that rebellious one may be fighting the reality of God's working in his or her heart. Don't run from that person; but like Stephen, stand your ground and witness for Christ.

Reality #2: God seeks a personal love relationship with you regardless. Three accounts of Saul's personal encounter with God appear in Scripture—in Acts 9, 22, and 26. In the last two accounts Saul gives his testimony in his own words. Each account has distinctive elements. In Acts 9, Jesus appears in a great light to Saul and says, "Saul, Saul, why are you persecuting me?" Not only was God at work around him, but God was showing His love through Jesus. God clearly was pursuing a love relationship with Paul when Jesus came face-to-face with him.

The amazing transformation in Saul was almost instantaneous. From one giving authoritative orders for the imprisonment of others, he became a submissive, obedient prisoner of Christ. As the light flashed around him and the voice sounded in his ears, he called Jesus Lord and asked to know more about Him. He took the energy he had used to murder disciples of the Way and turned it to prayer, fasting, and waiting on God. God worked in the lives of both Saul and Ananias to bring about the healing and restoration of this new brother. Within three days Saul's sight was restored, he was filled with the Holy Spirit, he was baptized, and he was proving to the Jews that Jesus was the Messiah.

Perhaps your encounter with the living Lord was not as dramatic as Paul's, but almost two thousand years later God still pursued you as relentlessly as he did Paul to draw you into a loving relationship with Him. He now pursues you to invite you to be on mission with Him to bring Christ to the unreached peoples of your day! Try to recall several ways that God has revealed His love for you as He has pursued you.

Do you remember what your first impulse was after Christ saved you? For most of us, that first impulse was to tell someone else about our experience. In the Acts 22:14 testimony, Saul repeats Ananias's words as he tells the three reasons God chose him: "to know His will," "to see the Righteous One," and "to hear the sound of His voice." All involve intimate relationships. God said, "I want an intimate relationship with you, and then you will be a witness of Me to all men of what you have seen and heard." The Lord desires the same of us today!

Reality #3: God's revelation is His invitation to go with Him. Through the obedient Ananias, Saul immediately knew his mandate from God to carry His gospel to the unreached people of his day. The Lord made His purpose in saving Saul crystal clear (Acts 9:15).

This revelation was Saul's invitation to be on mission with God—to take the gospel to the Gentiles, or all peoples. Even though the people of Paul's day did not understand the purpose for which the Lord had arrested him, Paul set out immediately to pursue God's goal for him. During his first attempts to preach in both Damascus and Jerusalem, the Jews tried to kill him—not once, but twice! Paul needed the guidance of the Holy Spirit to help him daily through the difficult transition from wicked oppressor to outstanding witness to the world.

Reality #4: God speaks by the Holy Spirit through the Bible, prayer, circumstances, and the church to reveal Himself, His purposes, and His ways. At every juncture in his life it was clear that Paul had a personal relationship with God and that God spoke to him. From the outset of his new life, Paul depended greatly on the Holy Spirit. This young Hebrew certainly knew the Scriptures, as his many epistles clearly show. He was a person of prayer who allowed the Lord to guide him using circumstances and counsel from other members of the body of Christ.

How has God been speaking to you? Do you keep seeing interesting Scripture verses that seem to relate to His invitation? Or does the same thought come to you again and again when you pray? Or are you seeing a coincidence in that different circumstances occur about the same thing that you have thought about them? Is it also possible that recently several people have confirmed a gift, skill, ability, or calling that you have? All of these could be God speaking to you.

Are you willing to embrace wholeheartedly God's will for your life, whatever it may be? Have you recognized the reason for which you have been saved—to be an instrument of God to reach the peoples who do not know Him? Saul embraced wholeheartedly the will of God for his life. He immediately began persuading the Jews that Christ was the Messiah.

Reality #5: God's invitation for you to work with Him always leads you to a crisis of belief that requires faith and action. Paul's first crisis of belief was during his conversion experience. During the three days in Damascus that he was blind, he didn't eat. This crisis of belief required faith and action. Everything that he thought he knew, he didn't know anymore. He did know one new fact, however—that he had met Jesus. Ananias said, "And now, what are you waiting for? Get up, be baptized." In this crisis Jesus told him what to do through someone previously unknown to Paul. When he obediently did so, God brought him right into the middle of His mission! However, those early days as a Christian would not end Paul's need to believe God. Four times Paul's alignment with God's will caused a crisis of belief and action (Acts 9:21–27, 29–30).

Reality #6: You must make major adjustments in your life to join God in what He is doing. Paul's whole life was one major adjustment—a more radical conversion than any other in the Scripture! The Lord showed Paul that it was a God-sized task to which He had called him (Acts 26:14–18). If he was to know the Lord's power resting on him, the old self-sufficient Paul needed to experience complete dependence on God. Nothing less would do on the mission God had for him!

Reality #7: You come to know God by experience as you obey Him and He accomplishes His work through you. The secret of Paul's success in facing suffering was his intimate relationship with the living Christ (Phil. 3:10). The more Paul obeyed, the more he experienced Christ. We don't need to recount here all the ways God used Paul.

PAUL'S WIDE-ANGLE LIFETIME EXPERIENCE

As dramatic as Paul's first experience with God was, it was his lifetime impact that we still feel today. Paul experienced God and along his path marked the milestones using Spiritual Markers.

Spiritual Marker #1: God chooses you to be on mission with Him to reconcile a lost world to Himself. At the outset of his Christian life, Paul was deeply impressed by God's assurance through Ananias that God had chosen him. Nothing could have been clearer than Paul's mandate from God. Yet Paul must have wondered, as you and I do, how God would work out the details. The Greek word for *chosen* that Paul uses in Ephesians 1:4 ("For He chose us in Him, before the foundation of the world, to be holy and blameless in His sight") pictures the idea that God "picked you out." As I mentioned earlier, it is as if God looked at a photograph and drew a circle around you. The same word is translated "chosen" in Acts 9:15, when God told Ananias that Paul had been chosen.

The idea that Paul was chosen was fixed in his mind by four factors (Acts 22:6–21): (1) In Damascus, Paul was told all that he had been assigned to do; (2) Paul knew that he was chosen to know God's will and to hear the Righteous One; (3) He was told he had been called to be the Lord's witness to all people; (4) Paul believed the Lord had told him He was sending him far away to the Gentiles.

Although God told Paul that he was chosen for His purpose, He did not tell him everything at once. Paul received a global glimpse of the reason God chose him, but he had to depend completely on the Holy Spirit for the day-to-day operation of His plan. God desires to build your trust in Him every step of the way.

Paul understood that we don't tell God what we are to do in life but that He makes us according to His purposes. Romans 9:19–21 in the Phillips translation gives us a clearer perspective on God's call. "When a craftsman makes anything he doesn't expect it to turn around and say, 'Why did you make me like this?' The potter, for instance, is always assumed to have complete control over the clay, making one part of the lump a lovely vase, and with another a pipe for sewage. Can we not assume God has the same control over human clay? May it not be that God, though He must sooner or later expose His wrath against sin and show His controlling hand, has yet most patiently endured the presence in His world of things that cry out to be destroyed?"

Which would you rather be: a Chinese Ming vase or a sewer pipe? Imagine how a sewer pipe would look with flowers in it atop a baby grand piano. Or how a plumber would feel if all he had were vases when he needed sewer pipes. Both items are exactly suited for their use. God will use you for the purpose He has chosen you.

Spiritual Marker #2: God calls you to Himself to go on mission with Him. Christians often look at their lives before they meet Christ to discern what God calls them to do. Although that may help, don't depend on it. With all Paul's training in the Scripture and experience in the Law, you would expect him to be called to witness to the scribes, Pharisees, and the Sanhedrin in Jerusalem. However, God sent him far away to the Gentiles, who didn't even know God. You would expect that God would call Peter, the rough fisherman, to go to the Gentiles, but instead He sent him to deal with the religious authorities in Jerusalem. God determines why He called you and what He wants you to do for Him.

You may rush to take personality tests or try to assess your skills, but when God calls you He distributes to you the spiritual gifts He wants you to have for your ministry. When an accountant is saved, church members often want to make him or her church treasurer. Of course, one can use that skill for the kingdom, but it is not a surefire way to know what you are called to do. Others may tell you, "You are a good speaker, so you are called to preach," or "You are a schoolteacher, so you should teach Sunday school." Rick Warren, in his book *The Purpose Driven Church,* gives a helpful acrostic, S-H-A-P-E, to help Christians get a balanced understanding of God's call. The words in SHAPE are Spiritual gifts, Heart or passion, Abilities,

Personality (type), and Experience. Apply the words in SHAPE to your life. When you look at all the aspects of your SHAPE, you get a balanced view of calling. God is sovereign; He will ultimately reveal to you what He has in mind. God made you unique in order to fulfill His mission through you. Ask Him to show you what He has called you to do.

Paul spent three years in Arabia and ten in his hometown learning what God wanted him to do. Finally, Barnabas went to Tarsus and invited Paul to Antioch to help him in the new Gentile church there. After Paul's year-long discipling experience with the Christians in Antioch (Acts 11:26), famine struck Judea, and he and Barnabas were sent to the elders in Jerusalem with a gift from the Antioch church (Acts 11:30). When they had proved themselves obedient, they returned to Antioch and continued faithful in worship and fasting before the Lord. While they were engaged in this activity with the elders of the church, the Holy Spirit spoke. This time He gave the next steps in God's purpose for them: "'Set apart for Me Barnabas and Saul for the work that I have called them to'" (Acts 13:2). Thus began the first of three missionary journeys that took Paul throughout the Roman world of his day. God calls you to be faithful in a little so that He may give you much to do for His glory.

The aspect of being called should be an integral part of the self-concept of every child of God. Your calling is based on God's grace, not on your ability. Keep on your toes watching to see what God wants to do through your life. Like Paul, you have been called to be on mission with Him!

Spiritual Marker #3: God initiates a covenant of promise and obedience with you. As you have seen throughout the Bible, God makes a covenant with those He calls. He told Paul, "I will rescue you from your own people and from the Gentiles." That's a promise. Paul had a lot of opportunities to prove that one—in dangerous situations in Ephesus and Corinth and suffering shipwreck on the way to Rome.

As you have already seen, Paul's obedience in his covenant connection with God brought him many hardships. However, he would be the first to admit that he was blessed above measure in his intimate relationship with the risen Christ. We are blessed to have his example to help keep our kingdom priorities straight!

Spiritual Marker #4: God prepares you for His mission. The Lord prepared Paul to be a witness and a servant to all peoples. When Paul was a young man, God sent him to school and let the Sanhedrin pay for it! He often lets the devil and the world pay for part of your education. He learned the Old Testament Scriptures. He got credentials that allowed him to step into any synagogue and people would say, "Speak to us, Paul." He spent three years in Arabia. He said, "I wasn't taught by any man; God taught me." God was reforming his whole heart and mind and preparing him to be that witness.

We don't know a lot about Paul's early ministry in the area of Galatia, but he served obscurely for ten years. Often God's choicest fruit ripens best in the shade.

Then one day Barnabas traveled the two hundred kilometers to Tarsus to find Paul and bring him back to Antioch. For a whole year, as they taught the church at Antioch, Barnabas discipled Paul, teaching him all about what had really happened in the first church and how things were to be done. Fourteen years of preparation occurred before Paul became prominent in ministry, and many experiences after that prepared him for the rest of his life. The bigger the job, the greater the preparation.

Modern Christians often forget suffering accompanies service. We need a fresh biblical theology of suffering in our day! Perhaps you have answered God's invitation to go on mission with Him, only to be met by discouragement and difficulties along the way. Be like Paul as you determine to endure and even embrace unfolding events.

As Paul obeyed God, Christ's character was formed in him through the sufferings he endured. The perseverance he learned led to this Christlikeness. Paul was ever hopeful and never disappointed because he expected to suffer in this life, knowing that he was sharing in His Lord's sufferings. Indeed, Paul learned to glory in his sufferings.

When you think life is the most difficult, God is actually getting you ready for a bigger job—to do something with you that you have not anticipated but that He has called you to do. Trials and tribulations toughen you spiritually so you will persevere under difficult circumstances!

Spiritual Marker #5: God sends you to the place where He can best work through you to accomplish His mission. From the beginning of his relationship with the risen Christ, Paul knew to whom he was being sent—the unreached, outcast peoples of his day. We will look in detail at this focus of his life later in the chapter.

Meanwhile, have you ever considered that you have the same privilege Paul had—reaching those who have never even heard the name of Jesus. Today six times more people have never heard of Christ than were alive when Paul went on mission with God! Some 1.7 billion people still do not even have access to the gospel.

To put that in perspective, if you could tell one person a second, it would take fifty-four years to share the gospel with them! In addition, another 1.4 billion are unreached by a gospel to which they may have technically had access but have not understood. Another 1.5 billion do not understand the gospel, although it has reached their countries and to some degree penetrated their cultures. That means that today, at least 4.6 billion people constitute the unfinished task!

How can we tackle such a gigantic job? Realize that God wants to use everyone on mission. You may be exactly where He can best work through you to accomplish His mission. These unreached people of the world may show up in your life as taxi drivers or supermarket clerks or as your next-door neighbors. Or God may have another destination. As you pray, has God directed your thoughts to a certain people or a certain part of the world? It may be the place He wants to send you to be His instrument, as Paul was during his lifetime.

Spiritual Marker #6: God guides you on His mission. God's guidance may be negative as well as positive. As Paul went west on his second missionary journey, the Holy Spirit prevented him from going north or south (Acts 16:1–10). So he continued in the last direction God had given him—west. When he got to the end of the land and waited by the Aegean Sea, Paul received a vision. From the vision and God's speaking he and the party with him concluded that God was calling them to another continent to preach—Europe instead of Asia. When they worked their way from Troas to Samothrace to Neapolis and finally to Philippi, they found a woman (not the man he had seen in the vision) whose heart the Lord opened to respond to Paul's message! God led him to the keeper of the prison (the man of Macedonia?) who asked, "What shall I do to be saved?" From this example, see that the way God guides is never stereotyped or boring. If Paul had allowed gender or Jewish prejudice to prevent him from preaching to Lydia, he would have missed God's will in this moment.

Can you recall an incident where God gave you partial instruction concerning a situation, followed by more information as you obeyed Him? God used many means to guide Paul. God spoke to Paul supernaturally through a vision or a trance. God also spoke directly to him and through an angel. He spoke through Ananias as a representative of the church. He used Barnabas and the apostles to convince him to leave Jerusalem. God used circumstances such as the Jews in Damascus and at Jerusalem wanting to kill Paul to convince him to leave. God guided Paul through prayer and fasting.

Paul lived a life so open to the Holy Spirit that he experienced continual guidance concerning His mission.

Perhaps in the past you have been confused or felt you did not have all the information you needed to follow the Lord. Do not allow personal prejudice or preconceived ideas to prevent you from doing the Lord's will. God guarantees you all the guidance you need when you need it. As you faithfully follow the light He gives you, He will provide more light. The path before you will unfold as you respond immediately to do His work in the way He chooses!

Spiritual Marker #7: God uses you to bring glory to His name. The apostle to the Gentiles played a major part in God's mission to peoples the Jews had failed to bless. When you realize that God also used Paul to write almost half of the New Testament, you can understand how God can use one person's life.

You may believe that you could never accomplish anywhere near what this apostle did during his lifetime. You may be right! But realize that Paul considered himself totally unworthy (1 Tim. 1:15). Gradually he learned to glory in his weaknesses, allowing God's strength to work through him (2 Cor. 13:9).

Although the apostle Paul worked tirelessly himself, he believed strongly in discipling and mentoring others to carry on the task of proclaiming God to all peoples. He rarely went on any part of a missionary journey alone but took with him at least one other person and often several. Paul sensed deeply the corporate nature of the church as Christ's body (Rom. 12:4; 1 Cor. 6:19; 12:12; Eph. 5:30). Paul taught the importance of team and body ministry and appointed elders in every church to equip the body to minister.

God will do His work with or without you. Wouldn't you rather He do it with you and through you? One way or another, God will bring representatives from every people group to worship Him and glorify Him. You are privileged to be chosen and called and promised and prepared and sent and guided and used to bring peoples to glorify Him for all eternity!

PAUL'S 180-DEGREE EXPERIENCE OF INFLUENCING ALL GOD'S PEOPLE TO BE ON MISSION

Rather than going through the process of how God used the Seven Spiritual Markers to influence the people of God through Paul's life, in this section I want to introduce how God used Paul to begin church-planting movements. These church-planting movements affected the people of God as they fanned out to start churches everywhere, but even more important, whole peoples were reached with the gospel in a short time.

God used Paul to teach the church about starting and nurturing church-planting movements among all peoples that will continue to reach out until all peoples will be reached. The best example of a church-planting movement occurred in Jerusalem after Pentecost where the believers numbered an estimated 100,000. But to see a church-planting movement begin without the one-of-a-kind Pentecost conditions, look at Paul's experience in Ephesus (Acts 19–20). Remember God prevented Paul from going to Ephesus and Asia earlier; the timing wasn't right (Acts 16:6–10). In time God led Paul back to Ephesus because He was ready to do something in the life of Paul and in Ephesus that would model for us a church-planting movement among the unreached. Paul's greatest impact on the corporate body of Christ was in the midst of starting church-planting movements.

Across the world today we are discovering how God is using church-planting movements to finish the task of the Great Commission in our day. I believe that God wants to start a church-planting movement in every people group. This may be a new concept to you, but it is biblical and represents the best way to reach the billions of people in the thirteen thousand people groups in the world. Only God can begin and sustain a church-planting movement, but He uses human catalysts to do so. As you read, ask God to allow you to be a part of a God-glorifying, church-planting movement in your area or among a people group with which you are familiar.

A church-planting movement is the rapid multiplication of indigenous churches among a people or population segment that enables them to spread the gospel among their people and to other peoples of the world. *Rapid* is a relative term, but by it I mean that the churches are multiplying new churches fast enough that you have a movement. This usually happens among a people—an ethno-linguistic group having its own culture and sense of "us" versus "them." To do this rapidly the churches must be indigenous—growing of themselves with their own language, culture, leadership, finances, and propagation without outside help.

God initiated a church-planting movement while we were serving in Indonesia. When we arrived a year earlier, this seemed unlikely. The Communists attempted a coup. Approximately 500,000 people were killed within the next three months. But in the aftermath, people started to see the Lord. Most of the churches doubled at least.[1] In just over five years, more than two million people were baptized into Indonesian churches. A church-planting movement began in a country where 85 percent of the people claimed to be Muslims! God can start these movements anywhere. I have seen church-planting movements also among peoples with animist, Hindu, and Buddhist backgrounds.

God's mission in Asia was bigger than Paul could see. At the right time God brought him where He needed him to be—in Ephesus—to start a church-planting movement that would spread throughout Asia Minor (Acts 19–20).

In assessing this situation, Paul discovered that the people were John's disciples and not Jesus' disciples (Acts 19:1–7). After he told them about Jesus and they believed in Him, he baptized them in Jesus' name. Then he prayed for them to be filled with the Holy Spirit. Paul spent three months teaching in the synagogue before they kicked him out. Then Paul took his disciples with him and had daily discussions in the lecture hall of Tyrannus. In one of the Bible's most amazing verses, Luke described what happened: "This went on for two years, so that all the inhabitants of the province of Asia, both Jews and Greeks, heard the word of the Lord" (Acts 19:10).

Did Paul preach to all of them? No. He stayed in the school of Tyrannus. He discipled the disciples to go make disciples and begin congregations of believers. He was the catalyst for a church-planting movement that spread the gospel all over Asia Minor. Here are the principles he used and taught the church.

1. *In a church-planting movement, someone has to go to the place where the people live, because the gospel will never get there unless an outsider takes it to them (Acts 19:10).* Paul asks, "How can they call on Him in whom they have not believed? And how can they believe without hearing about Him? And how can they hear without a preacher? And how can they preach unless they are sent?" (Rom. 10:14–15).

Michael Wright, pastor of Calvary Baptist Church of Tyler, Texas, challenged his people to adopt an unreached people group in India among whom there was no gospel witness. They had never personalized missions in this way but began to pray in earnest. Soon the congregation was electrified when Pastor Wright announced to the church that a couple from another church was considering going as missionaries to their adopted people. To support the couple in prayer, the church sent a contingent to the commissioning service before the couple left for India.

This praying church understands that someone from outside must first go to the people.

2. *In a church-planting movement, someone needs to research the situation to see what God has done and is now doing (Acts 19:1–4).* God had already prepared the way in Ephesus by having some of John's disciples make converts. God used John to prepare for Jesus in Palestine; He used John's disciples to prepare the way for the gospel in Ephesus.

A strategy coordinator began to focus on an unreached people group composed of ninety million people in North India. He discovered that the twenty-eight churches started by a Swedish missionary organization in William Carey's era had not started a church in more than twenty-five years. He first began advocating that they get out of their protective shell, caused by persecution, and reach out. He did not stop there. He mobilized other mission groups and denominations to begin evangelizing. Unfortunately some Christians used methods from South India that were highly offensive methods with this unreached people. Six evangelists were martyred before the Christians discovered how to evangelize among this people. As the strategy coordinator agonized over these events, God showed him where Jesus had told His disciples to find the man "of peace" in the villages where He sent them and to stay with him (Luke 10:5–7). Once they began following this biblical pattern among this people group, they began to see great results. In just twelve years the number of churches has grown from twenty-eight to more than four thousand!

3. *In a church-planting movement, someone must communicate the gospel (Acts 19:4–5).* Paul immediately began to preach on repentance and the gospel of salvation by faith. In this case

Paul already knew the language of the people—Greek. Among new people groups, worship is typically in the heart language of the people. While God's Word may be in another language that they can understand, it needs to be communicated in the heart language of the people—the one they love, cry, and get mad in—so worship is accessible to all and easily reproduced.

4. *In a church-planting movement, someone using the bridges God has provided has to move out of the group of believers to the people who need the gospel (Acts 19:8–10).* Paul always began in the local synagogue. He felt obliged to preach the gospel first to the Jews, but if they rejected it, he quickly moved on to the Gentiles. When a majority of the Jews in Ephesus rejected the message, Paul focused on the unreached Gentiles. In his book *The Bridges of God,* Donald MacGavran shows how God has developed "bridges" (or openings) from one people group to another over which the gospel may travel.

5. *In a church-planting movement, someone must find a neutral place to freely share the gospel and teach the disciples (Acts 19:9).* Tyrannus was probably a Greek philosopher who rented his hall to Paul. Public life in the Ionian cities ended regularly at the fifth hour (11 A.M.); thus the hall would be free for Paul to use the rest of the day. Following is a case study of a church-planting movement among the Kui people of Orissa, India.

A church-planting movement began among the Kui people of Orissa, India, in the 1990s. The Kui had begun to turn to Christ in 1914 when the British Missionary Society worked among them. A small, steady movement continued for several decades. But the BMS pulled out its missionaries in 1960, and growth plateaued for the next twenty years. International Mission Board missionaries began short-term training for leaders in 1986. From that, a remarkable awakening and church-planting movement exploded. In 1993, a lone agricultural missionary went in on a tourist visa and lived there for about two years, introducing agricultural methods to save and use the depleted land. The state government was impressed and appropriated two million dollars to make that method available all over the area.

While this was occurring agriculturally, the missionary decided to broadcast a fifteen-minute radio program in the Kui language twice weekly—the only Kui program on the air. The first seven or eight minutes focused on agriculture or public health. The second half focused on telling Bible stories. From this sprang the idea of "listener groups" for which 175 Indian believers were trained as leaders. They went to villages where no believers existed and gathered people to listen to the radio program and then discuss implications both for farming and for faith. Listener groups began developing into churches. More listener-group leaders were trained and entered other villages. In three years, the churches increased from two hundred to approximately nine hundred.

Today Kui worship style is totally indigenous. This has contributed to the spread of the gospel in the surrounding Khond Hills. The curriculum includes chronological Bible storying, or simple Bible content. As pastors are trained, they study public health, the Bible, and more storying as well as agriculture so they can help support themselves. In 1998, men came from a remote area of the Khond Hills with a petition from thirty-five hundred heads of households saying they wanted to become Christians. To date approximately 100,000 people, one-tenth of the Kui, have become Christians. They have already spread the gospel and begun church-planting movements among two other nearby people groups.

6. *In a church-planting movement, someone must make disciples (Acts 19:9–10; 20:17–25; 2 Tim. 2:2).* You can only have a church-planting movement when disciples are multiplied (Acts 20:20). Paul did the two things a missionary must do, preach and teach, where a missionary must do them—publicly and from house to house. Paul lived out the vision among them, taught them how to be shepherds, and built them up with the word of God's grace.

Although the apostle Paul worked tirelessly himself, he believed strongly in discipling and mentoring others to carry on the task of proclaiming God to all peoples. He rarely went on any part of a missionary journey alone but took with him at least one other person and often several. Paul sensed deeply the corporate nature of the church as Christ's body (Rom. 12:4; 1 Cor. 6:19; 12:12; Eph. 5:30). Paul taught the importance of team and body ministry and appointed elders in every church to equip the body to minister.

God used the need for discipleship to call me to return to the States and train disciplers. I developed *MasterLife: Discipleship Training for Leaders,* a small-group discipling process, which I wrote to help the churches multiply and reproduce disciples in the church-planting movement in Indonesia. In 1980, the first *MasterLife* workshop was conducted in the United States. One pastor who caught the vision for discipling led an initial group of ten persons in his church through the process. Five of those persons began new groups. One of the couples discipled over one hundred persons in the next four years including several overseas!

ON MISSION WITH GOD

A member of their first group felt led to attend seminary, where he led three groups. Those he discipled led six more groups in the next cycle. Here are five "generations" of disciples, each of which continues to multiply today around the world. *MasterLife* is being used now in more than fifty languages and over one hundred countries to develop disciples and leaders. Spiritual reproduction is a must in a church-planting movement.

7. *In a church-planting movement, someone must pray and expect God to do a supernatural work before those who oppose the gospel (Acts 19:11–17).* Paul prayed much and enlisted people in all the churches to pray for him. No church-planting movement ever began without prayer. As a result supernatural power was manifest to heal the people, for the evil spirits to be cast out, and for the people to burn their sorcery paraphernalia that was worth the daily wage of a laborer for 208 years! (Acts 19:18–20). In almost all church-planting movements, participants testify of supernatural miracles that happen and the people give the glory to God.

8. *In a church-planting movement, someone must equip multiplying leaders to lead the congregations (Acts 19–20).* We don't know how many churches began, but for everyone in Asia to hear the word of the Lord, it must have been thousands. We do know that the seven churches Christ addressed in Revelation 2–3 were part of the churches of Asia. When Paul came back, he called all the elders (what we call pastors today) from Ephesus to meet him at Miletus. In Acts 20, Paul tells how he equipped them to be multiplying leaders. Later Paul wrote the Book of Ephesians to train the whole church and leaders in particular. In Acts 20, you will find these seven principles Paul gives for multiplying leaders.

Multiplying Leaders

1. Multiplying leaders have a ministry themselves so they can model it.
2. Multiplying leaders care deeply for people.
3. Multiplying leaders communicate a vision.
4. Multiplying leaders involve disciples in the ministry.
5. Multiplying leaders train disciples in ministry skills.
6. Multiplying leaders delegate responsibility to disciples.
7. Multiplying leaders commission disciples as colaborers in ministry.

9. *In a church-planting movement, someone must equip disciples and leaders to multiply themselves and to multiply churches (Acts 19:10; 20:17).* If the missionary does it right, the churches will be indigenous, and they will on their own start other churches. Aquila and Priscilla, Paul's companions, helped start a church in their home and ultimately helped lead to phenomenal growth of the churches in Asia. Theirs was truly a first-century church-planting movement. Their church had no buildings but met all over town for worship and fellowship. As soon as disciples were equipped, they began new churches. They planned to move to Rome to start a church in their home as a beachhead for evangelizing the whole Roman Empire.

10. *In a church-planting movement, the leaders move on and let the indigenous leaders do the work, although the leaders retain a fraternal relationship with them, as Paul did (Acts 20:32–38).* Paul did the missionary's job—to be the catalyst for a church-planting movement and to train, model, and equip people who can carry out the Great Commission and then to back off. When you do that, God sets in motion through you something that can impact a whole people.

Today the Lord has put His people together in families called churches made up of fellow laborers. Beyond that, churches now organize themselves into denominations with mission agencies. Churches also work with parachurch organizations that focus on specific parts of the mission, such as Bible translation, *Jesus* film distribution, communications, literature, and service organizations. God has not called us to take on this God-sized task alone but has provided many colaborers in His harvest field, as He did for Paul.

THE 360-DEGREE PERSPECTIVE OF PAUL'S ETERNAL CONTRIBUTION

God's mission becomes crystal clear in His breathtaking revelation to Paul that all peoples will glorify God. He calls it "the mystery . . . [that] was not made known to people in other generations" (Eph. 3:4–5). God had to reveal it to Paul because the Jews had missed what God, throughout the Scripture, had said about including all peoples. From today's perspective you wonder how the Jews could have missed it. But you could also ask how the church today has missed the heart of God for all peoples and focused more on its own kind.

Paul's clearest expression of God's heart and, therefore, his heart for all peoples, is Romans 15. There Paul says his life message was all peoples glorifying God—a message that has become his eternal legacy to the body of Christ. God chose Paul to fulfill his divine destiny as the apostle to the Gentiles. Paul said that he was "one born out of due time," meaning that he should have been born earlier so he could have accompanied Jesus on earth as His other disciples did. But in God's plan, Paul was born right on time! He was to be the transitional leader from the apostles who had lived with Jesus and seen His glory to the rest of us who experience His glory by faith without sight. You, too, have been born at the right time in history for God to fulfill His eternal purpose through you.

Because Paul obeyed, God was able to accomplish His eternal purpose through Paul's life. Because he had a burning passion for eternal results, he allowed nothing to stand in the way of doing God's will. Often people make excuses or complain about circumstances, but not Paul. Paul knew God loved him and had a plan for his life, so he responded positively in all circumstances.

God doesn't just work in spite of circumstances; He works through them. When you face an obstacle or a disappointment, "give thanks in everything, for this is God's will for you in Christ Jesus," as Paul advised in 1 Thessalonians 5:18. God's Spirit will help you interpret circumstances and work through them to fulfill His purpose.

So, now, to the heart of the matter: What is the mission of God? You have studied this question for seven weeks. Open your Bible to Romans 15 and underline where Paul uses the phrase "so that" or "in order that" five times related to the mission of God.

They are signposts pointing to the purpose or mission of God—that all the peoples of the world glorify God! Paul makes his case by showing four reasons for the mission of all peoples glorifying God.

Eternal Truth #1: Christ gave His life so that all peoples would glorify God. "Now I say that Christ has become a servant of the circumcised on behalf of the truth of God, to confirm the promises to the fathers, and so that Gentiles may glorify God for His mercy" (Rom. 15:8–9). Here is testimony that God has been working throughout the Bible to this one end—that the Gentiles may glorify God! Now Jesus has become a servant of God's truth to confirm the promises made to the patriarchs beginning with Abraham.

Eternal Truth #2: The message of the entire Scriptures is that all peoples should glorify God (Rom. 15:4). Paul quotes four Old Testament Scriptures about the Gentiles (all peoples) in the verses that follow from four different perspectives (Rom. 15:8–12 NIV):

- A Testimony: "Therefore I will praise you among the Gentiles; I will sing hymns to your name" (from Ps. 18:49).
- An Invitation: Again, it says, "Rejoice, O Gentiles, with his people" (from Deut. 32:43).
- An Exhortation: "And again 'Praise the Lord, all you Gentiles, and sing praises to him, all you peoples'" (from Ps. 117:1).
- A Prophecy: "And again, Isaiah says, 'The Root of Jesse will spring up, one who will arise to rule over the nations; the Gentiles will hope in him'" (Isa. 11:10).

Paul presses home the point that God gave him to be the minister of Christ Jesus to the Gentiles (all peoples). He says that he has been called to offer up the offering of unreached people groups to God and urges the readers to join him in that sacred task (Rom. 15:15–16). If you believe the Scriptures, you, like Paul, will show it by your actions.

Eternal Truth #3: God desires for the unity of God's people so that He will be glorified among all peoples (John 17:20–24). "May the God of endurance and encouragement grant you agreement with one another, according to Christ Jesus, so that you may glorify the God and Father of our Lord Jesus Christ with a united mind and voice. Therefore accept one another, just as the Messiah also accepted you, to the glory of God" (Rom. 15:5–7).

All the desires of God's heart for the world hinge on the unity of His people. Obviously, God's desire for unity among Christians is so all the world will know Him.

How do we work together when we believe many different things and do things in different ways as churches, individuals, and organizations? Today Romans 15:5–7 is being fulfilled. But we have a long way to go in order for all of us to accept one another as Christ has accepted us. Only God can give us the spirit of unity so that we all can participate in His mission—that with one heart and mouth we may glorify the God and Father of our Lord Jesus Christ. Today God calls for a practical unity focused on the mission—that all peoples will glorify Him. We will not come together based on doctrinal distinctives or organizational models but on what is on God's heart—the nations.

When I first moved into my current job at the International Mission Board, I was concerned about my denomination's history and attitude of thinking we could win the world to Christ all by ourselves. I knew from my travels and experiences that God is at work among evangelical Christians all over the world, and not just among my own denomination. I wanted our denomination to partner rather than compete with Bible-believing evangelicals. While I was struggling with this matter, I was invited to speak on behalf of my denomination at the Global Conference for World Evangelization, a worldwide missionary gathering in South Korea sponsored by the A.D. 2000 and Beyond Movement in 1995. I apologized to other evangelical Christians for Southern Baptists' lack of humility and willingness to work with others. I confessed that too often we have ignored what God is doing through others and have thought that we could do alone what only the whole body of Christ can do—fulfill the Great Commission. I was stunned by the overwhelming support as we agreed to work together to fulfill the Great Commission in our generation.

God plans for the body of Christ to function together as a unit to reach the world for Him in this generation. If God makes you an eye, your primary function is not for you to see but to help the whole body to see. If He makes you a hand, it is not for you just to feed yourself but to help the body reach the lost. If you are a foot, you are not designed to take a walk by yourself, but you are to help the body walk to where God wants it to be. If you get frustrated and pull yourself out of the body, you deny the body the use of your gifts, and you end up without a body! If you go to the mission field as a Lone Ranger, the whole body doesn't get involved, and the world remains lost. If the whole body is to be marshaled for God's glory, you personally must adjust to God and patiently help your church adjust to God from top to bottom! Then you go on mission with God, and they "go with you."

Being on mission with God can do what all the councils that ever met, all the ecumenists who ever negotiated, and all the religious authorities who have ever tried to force unity could not do. The twenty-first century could be the time when Jesus' prayer is answered and Christians link arms as we march on mission with God to the last peoples on earth who do not know Him so that they can glorify Him and worship Him with us.

Eternal Truth #4: God calls missionaries so all peoples will glorify God (Rom. 15:15–24). Paul reminds us of what he had already mentioned—that God gave him grace to be a minister of Christ Jesus to the Gentiles. He then uses the analogy of a priest who had a duty to present an offering to God. His offering is the Gentiles who are accepted by God and sanctified by the Holy Spirit. He states his holy ambition to be a missionary pioneer who goes where no one else has ever gone with the gospel so that "those who had no report of Him will see, and those who have not heard will understand" (Rom. 15:20).

The statement in verse 23 is surprising because he says there is no more place for him to preach since he has fully proclaimed the gospel of Christ from Jerusalem all the way around to Illyricum. Does that mean that all those people have heard or understood the gospel? I don't think so. He means the gospel has been made accessible to them and that he has planted enough new churches that they will carry on the rest of the work of evangelization in those areas. He is still looking for the pioneer field, so he sets his sights on Spain. That is the essence of the missionary call—to proclaim Christ where the peoples have never heard or understood.

We have established that all Christians are to be on mission with God. We have said that they can be on mission in thousands of ways as God leads. However, God calls some people to be missionaries—to take the gospel across cultural and geographical lines. How would you know if you were called to be a missionary? Here are four ways you can know if you are being called to be a missionary:

1. You know you are called if God speaks to you through Scripture by impressing a passage or passages on your heart about being a missionary. Sometimes it comes in your quiet reading of Scripture, or the shout of a preacher, or the exciting testimony of a missionary.

2. You know you are called if God speaks repeatedly to you about being a missionary when you pray. You may be surprised how often God brings it to your mind when you pray. It might happen when you go to another country on a prayerwalk where you can pray "on site with insight."

3. You know you are called if God speaks repeatedly to you through circumstances. Circumstances alone are insufficient, but they do awaken you or confirm that you are called. Often people who go on short-term mission trips have a missions call confirmed or realize they are not called to that kind of ministry. God uses all kinds of circumstances to call you as a missionary.

4. You know you are called if God speaks repeatedly to you through His body, the church. When you ask godly leaders what they think about the possibility of your being a missionary, they will often endorse the idea. At other times someone may mention it to you. As you follow God's leadership, you will need the affirmation of God's people in many ways. Mission boards have

consultants who will dialogue with you about the requirements (such as references, medical exams, and gifts) needed for certain assignments. Sometimes one mission board will not accept you but another one will. If you feel called, peruse all avenues God opens to you.

You know you are called if God speaks to you about being a missionary in one or more of the ways that He speaks. God does sometimes speak in dramatic events as He did with Paul. But we have no such accounts of Silas, Timothy, or Titus being called dramatically. God also uses a process over time to slowly bring you to the realization that He is calling. If God calls you to be a missionary, you will be able to say with Bill Smith talking about church-planting movements, "It is a fun time to be a missionary."

8

JOHN ON MISSION WITH GOD

ALL PEOPLES WORSHIP GOD

"And the glory of the LORD will be revealed, and all
mankind together will see it. For the mouth of the
LORD has spoken."

—Isaiah 40:5

ONE SATURDAY MORNING WHEN I WAS TWENTY-ONE, I FOUND
A babbling brook in the San Bois Mountains of southeastern
Oklahoma. I sat on a rock and using my trusty *Nave's Topical
Bible* read all the Scriptures in the Bible about God's glory. It blew
my mind.

With Moses I saw the glory of God on a burning bush, in the
pillar of fire, in dark clouds on the top of Mt. Sinai, covering the
tabernacle, and finally the "backside of God" when Moses asked
to see God's glory. I gloried when God showed His power in the

storied plagues and the miraculous opening of the Red Sea so His children could leave slavery in Egypt and worship God freely.

In the second hour, I visited Solomon's temple through the mirror of Scripture when God's glory came down on the temple and all the priests rushed outside because God's glory was so overwhelming. With Isaiah I looked into heaven at God on His glorious throne and heard the Seraphims crying, "Holy, Holy, Holy, Lord God Almighty." On and on I read and pictured what was happening to these men as they experienced God's glory.

Somewhere during the third hour I beheld God's glory in Jesus on the mount of transfiguration and in His resurrection body outside the garden tomb. All morning long I felt the mounting crescendo of His glory rising within me until it exploded in Revelation 5:12–14 (NIV) with peoples of every tribe and language and people and nation singing in a mighty chorus:

"Worthy is the Lamb, who was slain
to receive power and wealth
and wisdom and strength
and honor and glory and praise!"
Then I heard every creature in heaven and on earth
and under the earth and on the sea, and all that is in them,
singing:
"To him who sits on the throne and to the Lamb
be praise and honor and glory and power
for ever and ever!"
The four living creatures said, "Amen,"
And the elders fell down and worshiped."

I could sit still no longer. I leaped to my feet shouting, "Glory, Glory, Glory!" I had not seen God's glory with my physical eyes like the men of the Bible, but I experienced God's glory. I had been introduced to the purpose of God's mission—that He would be worshiped and glorified by all peoples.

That experience helped me begin to see my life from God's perspective. We are looking from the inside out, and He is looking at us from the outside in. He sees our lives in full perspective, from beginning to end. And He sees how our lives fit together in His greater plan and purpose. It has helped me throughout the course of my life to try to see my life as God sees me.

John, "the disciple, whom Jesus loved," could never have imagined what God was going to do in him and reveal through him. One day he heard about John the Baptist, who sounded just like the prophet Elijah. He was sure God was working after he saw John in action and heard him preach about repentance! That must have been a shock to this young man!

JOHN'S CLOSE-UP VIEW OF EXPERIENCING GOD

Reality #1: God is always at work around you. You may think of John as a placid, contemplative individual, but the Bible paints a different picture of him as a young man.

He was the son of Zebedee and Salome, fairly wealthy people who owned a Lake Galilee fishing business big enough to require hired help as well as their sons' labor. John's mother later followed Jesus and generously helped provide for His needs. Her sons, James and John, were probably very much like her, determined and rather ambitious! They had fiery tempers, were vindictive toward those who rejected them, and were presumptive that they had power to call fire down from heaven (Luke 9:52–54). They were ambitious (Matt. 20:20–23) and possessive. So John was not a tender-hearted, loving individual, but God was at work in and around him.

Reality #2. God pursues a continuing real and personal love relationship with you. God fully pursued John from the beginning. He caused John to grow so fascinated with John the Baptist's preaching that he became his disciple.

John's interest in seeing God at work culminated in a dynamic encounter with the Son of God! John's disciples heard him say, "Behold the Lamb of God that takes away the sin of the world." They experienced God's glory as they watched John baptize Jesus in the River Jordan. They saw the dove descend and heard God's voice say, "This is my Son, whom I love; with him I am well pleased." An incredible encounter occurred when Jesus established His personal relationship with John and Andrew.

God's first step with us is to establish a personal relationship. Of the disciples, John felt he had the closest relationship to Jesus. He referred to himself as the disciple Jesus loved. That day John had a chance to begin to know Jesus personally and to ask Jesus questions about Himself and God's purpose in sending Him.

Reality #3: God invites you to become involved with Him in His work one revelation at a time. Soon Jesus took another step in this personal relationship with John; He came seeking John. John records Jesus' words, "My Father is still working, and I also am working" (John 5:17). John experienced the second step of a long journey when Jesus joined His Father at work and recruited the fishermen James and John to become fishers of men. He was not just giving them a fish; He would teach them how to fish!

Even though God relates to you personally, He has much more in mind than your personal experience. Read the following statement by missiologist Jeff Lewis and ask God what He has in mind for your life when He encounters you personally:

> Jesus is not our personal Savior. We live in a culture where personal means mine. You don't get a personal-pan pizza to share it or hire a personal trainer to share them, and you don't want everyone using your personal computer. Now don't get me wrong. I believe that you must receive Jesus personally and that one of the benefits of salvation is that we can have a personal and intimate relationship with the living God. But, Jesus is not our personal possessive savior, He is the "Savior of the world."[1]

Reality #4: God speaks to you to reveal Himself, His purposes, and His ways. John and the other disciples had the rare privilege of hearing God speak through the lips of His Son every day for three years. John also heard the voice of God speak at Jesus' baptism and on the Mount of Transfiguration. He heard God speak through the Old Testament Scriptures, particularly after hearing Christ teach about fulfilling them. He heard God speak to him in prayer, particularly while he was exiled on the Isle of Patmos.

John experienced circumstances throughout his life that echoed the voice of God. The Lord rebuked him for being too zealous and having the wrong motive in mind when John wanted to call down fire on the Samaritan town that rejected Christ. Another time He rebuked James, John, and their mother for asking the wrong question. The reason God speaks to you is to reveal Himself, His purposes, and His ways.

Reality #5: God's invitation for you to work with Him leads you on a bumpy road of crisis of belief. No doubt John and these other disciples felt strongly their obligations to family and financial concerns. After all, they were commercial fishermen. We know that Peter had a wife to support, and John and James certainly were an integral part of their father's fishing industry. Probably Zebedee had to hire two or three people to replace his sons after they dropped their nets and took off with Jesus! Major adjustments were required for everyone concerned in the lives of all the disciples of Jesus. Sometimes it costs others more than it does yourself when you follow Jesus. Faith is the answer when God asks the question, "Will you follow Me?"

Have you experienced a recent invitation from God that required you to believe Him and act immediately? James and John, Peter and Andrew followed Jesus at once when Jesus called them (Mark 1:16–20). The four fishermen were quick to respond, and it was not long before Jesus had them right in the thick of His ministry in Capernaum. Don't delay when God calls you to be on mission with Him.

Reality #6: You must make major adjustments when God calls you to join Him. Today, many distractions exist to doing the will of God. For you it may take a major adjustment in your career, your financial circumstances, the concerns of your parents, or any number of areas. No one who obeys the Great Commission has been able to avoid the necessary rearranging of priorities when God issues an invitation to join Him on mission. God may ask you to quit a good-paying job, to sell your house and car, to do additional study, to have a garage sale to rid yourself of accumulated "stuff," and generally to alter your whole lifestyle. Jesus could have argued with the Father about leaving the glory of heaven for a ministry as an itinerant preacher and as a sacrifice for sinful people. The disciples could have offered a dozen reasons not to leave all to follow Jesus, but they didn't stop to do that! They just got up and went, with no questions asked. Jesus' incredible magnetism called for unswerving loyalty on their part!

Separate the decision-making phase from the problem-solving phase. You may want to have all the problems solved before you make the decision. The Lord wants you to make the right decision; then He will help you solve the problems!

Reality #7: As you obey God, God accomplishes His purpose through you. John and the other disciples had many great experiences ahead of them as they went on mission with Jesus. Not all were pleasant. They ran into much opposition along the way. But what an experience and what an education they received from God's Son!

It is the same in your world. As God's Holy Spirit anoints and fills you, you will operate in God's power and authority to bring the good news to people. Those who have never known the concept of forgiveness will be astonished that such is available to them. I recently was present when a Hindu girl attended a Bible study for the first time in her life. Throughout the hour of discussion, she kept repeating that she couldn't believe forgiveness was being offered to cover all her sin. That concept was so foreign to her in her own religion that it was almost too good to be true! People all over the world are waiting for that same good news.

You have looked at John's initial experiences with Jesus and how he responded to the Lord. Perhaps you have had an experience with God and wonder what it will lead to. God has a design for your life, and that experience is one step in His grand design (Jer. 29:11).

A WIDE-ANGLE LIFETIME PERSPECTIVE OF JOHN'S EXPERIENCES WITH GOD

One lesson from the lives of the seven mentors that should be clear by now: Don't take an experience with God and camp there the rest of your life and miss what God has planned for you. The life of John is a good example of what God can do with ordinary people who join Him on mission for a lifetime. Let's see if we can learn some lessons by looking down on John's life from the vantage of the Seven Spiritual Markers.

Spiritual Marker #1: God chose you to be on mission with Him to reconcile a lost world to Himself. We know that God chose John long before Christ called him to join Him on mission. Jesus prayed all night before He summoned the disciples to follow Him. The Father communicated to the Son exactly who should make up that group of twelve. John was blessed to be chosen to that privileged relationship. God had a special purpose for Him. He was to be in the inner circle of Jesus' twelve disciples, along with his brother, James, and Peter. Beyond that, he became Christ's intimate friend, who reclined closest to Him at the Last Supper (John 13:25; 21:20). The crucified Christ commissioned him to look after His mother (John 19:26). John was even closer to Jesus than Jesus' own family members!

Christ didn't allow John to grow close to Him just for John's benefit. The Lord's focus was on reconciling a lost world to God. Because John was so close to Him, he could hear Jesus' heartbeat for the world. John was chosen to live a long life (at least ninety years) so he could impact the world more with Christ's message of reconciliation. You have been chosen for the same incredible purpose! God will use you in the unique way He has planned for your life as you go on mission with Him.

Spiritual Marker #2: God calls you to Himself to be on mission with Him. God's call is not to a position or a program but to intimate fellowship with Him. As one called to be a part of the inner circle with Jesus, John experienced the joy of observing His Lord at close range under all kinds of circumstances. On certain occasions John, James, and Peter were present when the other disciples were excluded. No doubt the Lord had a special purpose in mind for the part they would play in His kingdom (Mark 5:34–43).

You have the incredible opportunity of being Jesus' intimate disciple today. He calls you to help Him complete His task. God confirms His choice of you when you recognize His call and follow Him. You choose the level of intimacy you want to have with Him! As I look back, I realize that the times I actually worked with my earthly father were the times I got to know him best.

Spiritual Marker #3: God initiates a covenant of promise and obedience with you. Have you ever been offered a job situation that was too good to turn down—more money, a bigger expense account, prestige, perks, and the works? On that memorable day when Jesus called John to follow Him, He promised him something that money could not buy.

231

Then, with a word, Jesus changed his whole career. Jesus didn't have a contract for John to sign, guaranteeing him a certain wage for the work he would do in God's kingdom. But He gave him a promise. Great courage and faith were necessary for John to leave everything behind, including his father and a comfortable lifestyle. Catching people would be hard work, but it was much more important than just catching fish!

Perhaps the Lord has called you to leave behind everything at which you have become skilled in order to be on mission with Him. He may ask you to leave a comfortable lifestyle or your parents' home for a much less certain existence that doesn't even guarantee a minimum wage! John didn't stop and count the cost, nor did he cling to his creature comforts. He was drawn by the magnetic personality of the Lord and by the urgency of His mission to a lost world of men and women dying in their sin. The Lord called him to a lifetime commitment of obedience and faith, promising him an eternal reward for his faithfulness. John made that covenant with Christ and, having put his hand to the plow in the kingdom of God, never looked back!

Perhaps Jesus has called you to use your skills and relationships right where you are to fulfill His mission in the world. Perhaps He is telling you to cut back to a simpler lifestyle and give the difference that others might have eternal life. While reading this book, have you come to the place where you would be willing to leave whatever to follow Christ: your career, your family, a comfortable home, your close friends, a good salary, your church or your country? Remember the formula:

COVENANT = PROMISE + OBEDIENCE = BLESSING!

Spiritual Marker #4: God prepares you for His mission. Jesus knew the disciples needed His character formed in them before they were prepared to carry out His commission. For three years He set them an example of love, humility, servanthood, obedience, faithfulness, and suffering which they would long remember. He discipled and mentored John and the others to build these characteristics into their lives. He commanded them to wait in Jerusalem until the Spirit came upon them in power. After that experience, they were never the same again!

Evangelist D. L. Moody was preaching to great crowds when two elderly women said to him repeatedly, "We are praying for you." Finally he asked them what they were praying in his behalf. They said, "We are praying that you will be filled with the Holy Spirit." Moody was miffed that they thought he wasn't filled with the Spirit, but something in his spirit prompted him to listen. He talked with them further, and that began his search for the filling of the Spirit. A few days later as he walked down the street in New York City, the Spirit of God fell on him and revealed Himself to Moody. He said, "I had such an experience of His love that I had to ask Him to stay His hand." After experiencing God's glory, the difference in his ministry after that was that Moody was used to bring hundreds of thousands to the Lord, instead of a few hundred. At that point, his whole ministry was completely changed.[2]

Reading Moody's story was the turning point in my life. I recognized how much I needed to be filled with the Spirit. Anything that has happened in my life is because the Spirit did it, not because I did it. In those early days after that experience, I told the church that I pastored, "If I don't show up some Sunday, it's because I'm not filled with the Spirit. If I am not filled with the Spirit, I don't have anything to tell you. So if I don't show up, you pray for me." I always showed up, but I had some close calls. I sometimes had to do some fervent praying before I got up in the pulpit. God wants to fill you with His Spirit because it is the Spirit of God who is the power and who does the work!

John experienced the filling of the Spirit and was prepared for everything the world could throw at him.

Spiritual Marker #5: God sends you to the place where He can best work through you to accomplish His mission. God had planned for John to have a big role in His mission. He would be imprisoned and beaten for his faith. Herod would behead his brother, James. He would be asked to go to the outcast Samaritans to examine those who had believed. Finally he would be exiled to the island of Patmos, where he would have a revelation of Christ that he would write as the last book of the Bible. What kind of preparation would Jesus have to give John so he could do what God had planned for his life? Certainly more than John could have ever imagined.

Have you ever been frustrated because someone asked you to do a job and you had no idea how it fit into the bigger scheme of things? God tells you what you need to know when you need to know it. Jesus carefully monitored the progress of John and His other disciples and gave them more responsibility, as they were faithful in the small tasks.

Jesus prepared John for his ministry after Pentecost and his exile on the island of Patmos. Step by step, John moved gradually from "acquaintance" to "friend" of Jesus: John was sent out with the other disciples early in Jesus' ministry to preach the gospel and heal people from village to village. He took part in the feeding of the five thousand. He, with James and Peter, was privileged to be on the Mount of Transfiguration and meet Moses and Elijah as he saw Jesus glorified. He needed correction from Christ when he tried to stop someone driving out demons in Jesus' name. He was rebuked when he and his brother wanted to call down fire on a Samaritan village. He and James drew indignation from other disciples when their mother requested special places in Christ's kingdom for her two sons. Jesus reprimanded him in Gethsemane for sleeping when he should have been praying.

God looks for dependable people to be His friends, so when He sends them out, He can depend on them. Jesus told John and the other disciples, "You are My friends if you do what I command you. I do not call you slaves anymore, because a slave doesn't know what his master is doing. I have called you friends, because I have made known to you everything I have heard from My Father" (John 15:14–15). In the normal course of events, a servant doesn't understand what the master has in mind. A servant is usually told to go plow the back forty acres or mop the floor or prepare lunch. He expects no thanks. He has done his duty (Luke 17:7–10). Jesus says, "I'm not just commanding you to go do a job. I call you friends because I have told you the Master's business. Everything I learn from My Father I have made known to you." What is the Master's business? The Master's business is producing fruit through His disciples that will last, so that He may reap an everlasting harvest through them! (John 4:34–38; 15:14–16; 17:4). The Lord desires to produce fruit through you as He sends you on a lifetime quest for His kingdom!

Spiritual Marker #6: God guides you on His mission. John became a faithful friend and dependable disciple as the Lord guided him throughout his lifetime. He partnered with Peter to become an effective team player as God led them into various circumstances. John was with Peter and James in the garden of Gethsemane as the Lord called on them to pray during His agony (Mark 14:33). Through John's influence, Peter was permitted into the high priest's courtyard as Christ was led to trial (John 18:15–16). Mary Magdalene found the two together when she ran to tell them of the resurrection, which means that John befriended Peter even after his infamous denial of the Lord. The two ran to the tomb together to check out Mary's story (John 20:2–9). After Christ's ascension, the Lord guided them to testify before the Jewish rulers of the day. Standing before the Sanhedrin, they did not flinch. Commanded not to speak or teach in Jesus' name, Peter and John, guided and empowered by the Holy Spirit, replied: "Whether it's right in the sight of God for us to listen to you rather than to God, you decide; for we are unable to stop speaking about what we have seen and heard" (Acts 4:19–20). As an old man, exiled to Patmos for his faith in Christ, John endured loneliness and suffering without complaint (Rev. 1:9).

Can God really depend on you to obey as He guides you? If you say, "I am obedient most of the time," does that mean 65 percent of the time, or 70, or 80 percent? How much can you trust someone who is dependable some of the time? What if you sent him on a mission during the 15 percent of the time he was undependable? An unfaithful man is like a lame foot in times of trouble (Prov. 25:19). You can't depend on somebody unless he or she is faithful and obeys consistently. God doesn't expect perfection, but He does expect faithfulness.

Spiritual Marker #7: God uses you to bring glory to His name through His mission. As you see John's development over his lifetime, does it inspire you to hope that you can be used effectively in God's kingdom? Watching this young "Son of Thunder" is fascinating as He is transformed into the "apostle of love." As Jesus looked from the cross at this disciple whom He loved, He knew that John had the potential to become a pillar in the Jerusalem church, a bishop of the church at Ephesus, and a writer of four books of the New Testament. As he continued to follow the Lord obediently, John's character was transformed, and he was able to shoulder the responsibility God had prepared for him. No doubt his daily concern for Christ's mother prepared him for the care he would have to exercise for the churches over which he was given oversight. In his later years, his main theme was love, which he exemplified, in great measure. Today, God uses imperfect Christians just as He used the imperfect John.

THE 180-DEGREE PERSPECTIVE OF HOW GOD WORKED THROUGH JOHN TO INFLUENCE HIS CHURCHES TO BE ON MISSION

Now let us move beyond John's lifetime to focus on John's influence on the church. As you study John's influence, think about your influence on your present church and any other churches to which God leads you. God revealed the Book of Revelation last because it is directed to the churches of the last days. As time passed, the love of many had grown cold. They were no longer on mission with God. They needed a fresh word from God and a challenge to join Him on mission. No doubt John reflected on the Great Commission that God had given so many years before. Although the gospel had spread to many places, it was not reaching to the uttermost parts because the churches were not on mission with God any longer. In Jesus' revelation to John, Jesus walks among the churches and speaks to their pastors. I believe God told John what to say to them to address the many kinds of situations that His churches face today. His return to earth is at any time. He comes through the Holy Spirit every day and speaks through His messengers about the church's condition. God is concerned about His people because His mission through them requires a relationship with Him.

As a child, did you ever build a big sand castle at the beach, only to watch the incoming tide wash it away? John must have felt somewhat like that as he saw the first-century heresies taking their toll on the church of Christ. The seven churches of Asia Minor, especially the one at Ephesus where he had been bishop, were dear to him. Their weakened condition grieved him. The One who holds "the keys of death and Hades" spoke to His corporate body through John and showed them the remedy for their condition!

Jesus visits His churches personally. Jesus walks among the lamp stands that symbolize the churches and holds in His hand the stars that represent His messengers. He gives a message to John for the messengers or pastors of the churches. When John first saw Christ as He prepared to walk among the churches, he was stunned (Rev. 1:10–18). He saw Christ glorified before him and fell at His feet as if he were dead!

Slow down reading for a moment. Relive John's experiencing God's glory, in exile on Patmos, as he worshiped the Lord one Sunday. First he heard a loud voice like a trumpet. He turned around quickly and the first thing that caught his attention was one "like a son of man" dressed in a white robe with a golden sash around his chest. He saw Christ walking among seven golden lamp stands (representing the seven churches). John noticed that His head and hair were white as snow and His eyes were like blazing fire. I think that he could not look continually into those blazing eyes and dropped his eyes to the ground, because the next thing he mentioned is Christ's feet that were like bronze glowing in a furnace. Suddenly he heard Christ's voice like the sound of rushing waters. At that he looked up and saw Christ's hands, which held the seven stars representing the churches. His eyes inched up to Jesus' face, and he saw the sharp double-edged sword coming out of His mouth. That's when he fell to the ground as if he were dead.

How will you feel when you meet Christ face-to-face? Every account in the Bible shows people overcome by His presence! (Judg. 6:21–23; Isa. 6:1–5; Ezek. 1:28; Luke 5:8).

Christ spoke to the pastors of the churches. He commended the churches for some things but condemned them for others and warned them of impending judgment if they did not repent. What would Christ say to today's churches? What does He say to your church? Use these seven examples to evaluate how the people of God you know and are a part of fare as Christ walks among us.

Corporate Reality #1: God says, "To be on mission with Me, return to your first love" (see Rev. 2:1–7). The church at Ephesus had many strengths and weaknesses. The many strong qualities of this church are completely counterbalanced by the major weakness—loss of their first love for the Lord. Only thirty-five years earlier Paul had written to commend them for their faith and love (Eph. 1:15–16). How far they had fallen in just one generation!

Today the corporate body of Christ suffers from the same disease. Over 70 percent of the churches in the United States have been plateaued for years. For the United States to have the same ratio of churches to its population it had in 1961, it would need to add ninety thousand new churches! If Satan can tempt your church to leave its first love for God, he has won the victory in your life.

What did Jesus mean by "your first love"? First, He meant their personal, intimate relationship with Him. Second, He meant their love for the lost and dying world. You demonstrate your love for Christ by your actions to people. God is not so much interested in your words as your actions. He knows when you are not thrilled by experiencing His glory in worship, fervent in prayer, eager to tell others of your love, focused on Him during worship, intensive as you talk about Him, focused on His mission more than your own, and seek His glory more than your own.

If you fail at love, you fail absolutely. The remedy for this church's situation was twofold: remember and repent. Christ reminds the members of the "height" of their first experience of love for Him (Eph. 3:16–21). No other remedy existed for them but to repent and do the things they did at first—in simple terms, love and obey Him.

How much is your church like the church at Ephesus—lacking in love for our Lord? Repentance was the key to the revival of their relationship with Him. Repentance means you and your church turn back and do what He commands. Real and lasting spiritual awakening will occur only through prayer and obedience, the heartbeat of revival. Stop now and pray until:

- You are aware of God's presence.
- God's presence and holiness awe you.
- You are alarmed by His convicting call.
- You are awakened to your first love.
- You repent and return to Him.

In the process you may hear a clarion call that reveals God's impending judgment on your church and how He views it, as the church at Ephesus did. Christ's promise to those who were overcomers—those who obeyed Him—was that He would give them the right to eat from the tree of life in the paradise of God. With that eternal prospect in view, you have great incentive to overcome your lethargy in the Christian life and return in repentance to the white-hot heat of your first intimate love for Christ.

Fire symbolizes this kind of love. Here are some aspects of fire that relate to your relationship with the Lord:

- Fire always starts from an outside source. (God alone can set your heart on fire for Him or the lost.)
- Fire must always have new fuel to burn. (You must be relating to God in daily Bible study to keep on fire for Him.)
- Fire must have oxygen to burn. (Prayer is the oxygen of the soul. Your daily prayer life, or lack of it, will cause it to blaze or cool off.)

Jesus gives you the remedy for your situation, just as He did the church at Ephesus—remember and repent, asking Him to rekindle your love for Him! Enlist others in the corporate body to pray with you and for you. Then be on mission with the Lord in your church to share the message of revival and spiritual awakening with others who need it. Remember: revival always begins in a single heart and spreads through His body to the world.

Corporate Reality #2: God says, "To be on mission with me, stay faithful unto death" (see Rev. 2:8–11). The church at Smyrna faced suffering on every side. Members experienced afflictions and poverty as well as slander and persecution. But Christ considered them rich in such circumstances, because their faithfulness in severe trials would earn them a crown of life. On top of that, He promised those who were overcomers that they would not be hurt by the second death, which would separate them from God forever.

Many believers and churches in Third World countries face such persecution today. One young Muslim believer in North Africa was savagely beaten for his faith. He had read the Bible to refute it with the teachings of the Koran but instead had been led to salvation in Christ through its pages. Then he began to write a book to refute the Koran. Later, some fundamentalist Muslims from the group he had once been a member of arrived at his home while he was out. His mother showed them his writings. They found and beat him mercilessly. In the hospital, he cried out again and again, "They're trying to kill me." However, the doctor in the emergency room told him he no longer needed to fear the three men he had named who beat him because they had been pronounced dead on arrival at the emergency room earlier because of an automobile accident. The believer is now writing books to prove Jesus is the Son of God.

Christ knows the situations His faithful ones face. He has endured great suffering for them and set an example of overcoming the evil one. He is standing with them in every trial, even as He stood by John as he suffered persecution and exile. American Christians are so sheltered that they don't often think of the possibility of physical persecution in their lifetime. Prejudice, persecution, the shootings of believers in churches and schools, and terrorist attacks in America have made us more attuned to that prospect. Persecution will someday be the norm for the corporate body of Christ all over the world. Be prepared to be an overcomer, no matter what the circumstances.

Corporate Reality #3: God says, "To be on mission with Me, you must be pure in doctrine and life" (see Rev. 2:12–17). Have you ever felt uncomfortable around someone who seemed to be able to see right through you? Perhaps a parent or teacher or someone else who knew you well could, with a look or a word, penetrate to the heart of what you were thinking or doing! The church at Pergamum must have felt the same way when it realized that the Lord knew its deficiencies. Members of this church were to experience "the sharp, double-edged sword" of His mouth, which spoke directly to their condition. Even though members of this body of Christ remained true to His name and did not renounce their faith when one of their numbers was martyred, major problems required their attention. Heresies enticed the church people to live ungodly lives. Again the Lord called them to repentance, promising the overcomers rewards of hidden manna and a white stone with a new, individual name written on it.

Modern-day heresies have sapped the strength of many churches. Many have watered down the gospel and allowed New Age thinking to crowd out Christ's claims. Others tolerate blatant sexual practices which God's Word condemns. Universalism ("In the end all people will be saved."), relativism ("There is no absolute truth."), humanism ("We can do it alone."), secularism ("Leave God out of this."), and sensualism ("If it feels good, do it.") are heresies which prevent many churches from being on mission.

Only truth will keep you doctrinally pure in this day when the edges of everything are blurred. As a well-taught student of the Word, you can be a catalyst to keep the church of Jesus Christ holy until He comes again for His bride!

Corporate Reality #4: God says, "To be on mission with Me, stop tolerating sexual immorality" (see Rev. 2:18–29). The church in Thyatira had many good qualities, but it also had an outstanding weakness. Immorality was rampant, and members refused to deal with a situation requiring discipline. The One "who searches hearts and minds" and would repay each according to his or her deeds was well aware of their condition, however, and required an accounting. Intense suffering was ahead if they were unwilling to repent. Some were not led astray, however, and the Lord promised to give them authority over the nations and the morning star.

Today many churches are unwilling to take disciplinary actions when people refuse to repent of immorality and other serious sins that quench God's fire. No wonder many churches are cold and lifeless! Ask what your church's disciplinary policy for serious sin

244

is. And be sure that you personally have a spiritual friend who will hold you accountable for sexual purity.

Corporate Reality #5: God says, "To be on mission with Me, you must wake up" (see Rev. 3:1–6). A ninety-foot tree that looked perfectly healthy once fell across my car in the driveway. The hidden root system deteriorated to the point it couldn't withstand the winds that toppled the tree. That tree was like the church at Sardis. It appeared to be alive, but the Lord saw that it was dead. He saw what remained needed strengthening, particularly in the area of deeds. He admonished members to remember, obey, and repent. To the few who were spiritually alive, He promised the privilege of walking with Him in white garments. The overcomers in the Sardis church would never have their names blotted out from the book of life.

Your church may be like the church at Sardis—full of activity and programs but lacking in spiritual power. Many churches in the corporate body of Christ try to do His work in their own strength.

Christ loved the Sardis church and wanted to see it restored to its former vitality. That could only occur as members sought spiritual awakening through prayer. Encourage your church to pray regularly for revival and spiritual awakening. Become a catalyst for your church's spiritual awakening, if needed.

Corporate Reality #6: God says, "To be on mission with Me, you must enter the open door" (see Rev. 3:7–13). The church of "brotherly love" at Philadelphia seems to be the only one that Christ highly commends. Members appear to have loved and obeyed Him to a greater degree than those in any of the other six churches. Their one weakness seems to be in the area of strength;

they have little of it! Even under those conditions, they have kept His Word, have not denied His name, and have obeyed His command to endure patiently. The rewards for this were an "open door" placed before them, acknowledgement by those in the synagogue of Satan that they are beloved by God, and the promise that they would be kept from the hour of trial that would test the whole world. They are admonished to hold on to what they have, so that their crown will not be taken away. The overcomers will be made pillars in the temple of God, and they will have the name of God, the New Jerusalem, and Christ written on them. This church was obviously on mission with God, impacting the pagan world around it. It had not stopped depending on the Spirit of God, so He was opening a door of opportunity for this church that no one could shut.

Corporate Reality #7: God says, "To be on mission with Me, you must let me in" (see Rev. 3:14–22). The "lukewarm" Laodicean church was hypocritical. Members said they were rich and needed nothing, but Christ saw them as wretched, pitiful, poor, blind, and naked. The Lord seems to be exhausting adjectives to adequately describe them! They boasted of their own accomplishments but could not see their desperate spiritual condition. Christ had what they needed if they would only humble themselves and pray and seek His face and turn from their wicked ways. He could give them refined gold, white garments to cover their nakedness, and eye salve to view themselves as He saw them.

The Lord's unconditional love is evident in His willingness to rebuke and discipline them. Their immediate need was to be earnest and repent. Obviously they ignored their relationship with Him to the point that He felt like an outsider, having to knock to gain admittance to their hearts. Revelation 3:20 was not written to the lost but to the saved! "Listen! I stand at the door and knock. If anyone hears My voice and opens the door, I will come in to him and have dinner with him, and he with Me."

Pray that God's Holy Spirit will ignite your heart and cause the light of your life to burn brightly so all may see it and glorify your Father in heaven! Remember that John's message was to the pastors of the churches. Pastors are responsible for telling the churches what Christ is saying about them. All Christians are responsible for praying that their pastors will be faithful to the True Shepherd for and responding to Christ's call for repentance. You and I cannot bring about biblical revival and the spiritual awakening to which God is calling us. Only God can do it! But He has told us our part is to get right with Him and join Him on mission.

THE 360-DEGREE PERSPECTIVE OF JOHN'S ETERNAL CONTRIBUTION TO THE MISSION OF GOD

You may have felt that the last section was a diversion from the main thrust of this book. But it is at the heart of it. We stand in danger of failing to join God on mission as the Jewish people whom He called to be servant priests to the world did. Once we get right with God, we will be dazzled by the glory of God!

As we move toward the conclusion of our bird's-eye view of the Bible, what do you think the Bible is all about? Before reading further, close your eyes and try to answer that question for yourself. The panorama that we have been studying from God's perspective leads us to these inevitable conclusions:

- The Bible is all about God's mission in time and eternity.
- God is revealing Himself to all peoples.
- God wants all peoples to know Him, His name, and His glory.
- God loves all peoples and is willing to make the ultimate sacrifice of His Son on the cross to redeem them.
- God's mission will result in the knowledge of His glory covering the earth as the waters do the sea.
- God's eternal kingdom will include representatives of all peoples glorifying Him forever.
- God has invited us to be on mission with Him, be involved in establishing His eternal kingdom, and reigning with Him throughout eternity.
- It's all about God and His glory!

Have you ever skipped to the last page of a good book just to see how things would turn out? As you look at the end of time as Revelation describes, the final scene around the throne is fascinating! How exciting to realize that God's vision of history's final scene concludes the assignment begun with Abraham to bless all the peoples of the world!

Now let's look at God's eternal perspective on the final goal of His eternal mission.

Eternal Reality #1: God will use His people to bring representatives from every people group to worship Him. Even though Abraham and all the heroes of the faith you have read about were unable to see the outcome of their obedience, God used their faith-filled lives to advance to a specific end—the scene before you in Revelation. God invites you to join Him by faith (Heb. 11:39–40). To experience God's glory on mission with Him requires that you walk by faith, not by sight.

From the first century, in which John lived, the Lord has built His church in miraculous ways. As the apostles fanned out and witnessed and discipled all nations, God began sweeping many people into the kingdom. In a similar way, God is working today in unusual ways in many places, calling people to Him.

For example, in 1900, only 3 percent of all the African people were Christian. Today Africa is 46 percent Christian, and Christians will soon be the majority. In 1900, in Latin America, fewer than forty thousand evangelicals existed. Today, almost forty million are evangelical. Asia had about sixteen million Christians in 1980. Today we can count more than one hundred million. You and I have been given the best opportunity in all of history to reach those whom God desires to call to be a part of His corporate body. Every year new people groups hear the gospel for the first time, begin churches, and multiply the witness to all their people. Remember the church-planting movements we saw Paul start. Hundreds of thousands are coming to Christ every year! Thirty thousand Chinese come to Christ every day!

Eternal Reality #2: God will fulfill His mission so that all peoples will worship Him. From the beginning of Genesis, God has been behind the scenes propelling history toward the compelling conclusion of Revelation. The apostle John was privileged to see the culmination of redemptive history. His thrilling report allows you to observe a wonderfully triumphant scene around the throne of God in heaven! (Rev. 5:9–10; 7:9–10; 14:6–7; 15:4). People from every nation, tribe, and language stand before the throne. The ancient promise made to Abraham and his heirs is fulfilled. As history comes to an end, John tells us that the "blessing" has indeed reached all the peoples of the world!

From Abraham, through Moses and David, Jesus, Peter, Paul, and John, you have now observed the beginning, middle, and end of His story. He made a promise. He made an oath. He made a way through the redemptive work of Jesus so that you may play an important part in the fulfillment of His mission. You can stand around the throne of God rubbing shoulders with individuals who have heard through you the good news that rescued them from the kingdom of darkness.

The mission to bless all the peoples of the world is God's plan to bring all peoples into the family of God. The final scene of history is not a throng of individuals standing before the throne recounting their blessings one by one. Rather, it is a scene of all the peoples of God—a family drawn from every language, tribe, and people—giving honor and glory to the rightful Lord over all.

Today God is initiating work around this world as never before. Do you realize the number of people who are alive today with the possibility of hearing the gospel? It took from the time of creation until 1830 to get the first billion people in the world, all alive at one time. It took another one hundred years to get the second billion, by 1927. It took another thirty-four years, to 1964, to get the third billion. It only took fourteen years to get the fourth billion. In October 1999, the world surpassed six billion, and it's still escalating. That means that possibly more people are alive today than have lived through the ages! God has given us enormous opportunities.

Eternal Reality #3: Eternity is the fulfillment of His eternal plan. God blesses His people so that they will in turn bless all peoples. Because He loves His creation and wants its highest good, God desires that all people worship Him with all of their being throughout the endless ages. He welcomes the untold billions of His creation to be blessed guests at the marriage supper of the Lamb. There they will worship Him forever and ever and be blessed by His presence with them always!

The world will not be won to Christ with "business as usual." As you go on mission with Him, are you willing to do new things, break old paradigms, and work in every possible way with your brothers and sisters in the body of Christ to get the gospel out today to those who have never worshiped Him? Are you willing to change the question from, What can I do? to, What will it take to reach all the peoples of the world?

Eternal Reality #4: All peoples will worship God. John Piper says, "Missions is not the ultimate goal of the church. Worship is. A mission exists because worship doesn't. Worship is ultimate, not missions, because God is ultimate, not man."[3]

"The great sin of the world is not that the human race has failed to work for God so as to increase His glory, but that we have failed to delight in God so as to reflect His glory, for God's glory is most reflected in us when we are most delighted in Him.

"God is calling us above all else to be the kind of people whose theme and passion is the supremacy of God in all of life. No one will be able to rise to the magnificence of the missionary cause who does not feed on the magnificence of Christ. There will be no big world vision without a big God."[4]

251

Piper's insightful statements bring us to the throne, but I want to go one more step beyond his statement that worship is the ultimate goal of the church; that is, God is the ultimate goal! Worship is our means to that end. I agree with Piper that failing to delight in God's glory is the human race's greatest sin. When He is your focus, your joy, your satisfaction, then you overflow and want to increase His glory. I also agree with Piper's third quote, that God calls you to feed on the magnificence of Christ. He is your vision, and His being glorified by all peoples is so much bigger when you see and worship Him. So He is the fuel of missions and the center of your life.

Every day you face hundreds of decisions of one kind or another. You are pulled, you are distracted, and sometimes even in your best moments, you don't get to what is ultimate. Even focusing on experiencing the glory of God is one step short of focusing on God. So neither missions nor worship is ultimate—God is. You can get enamored with a telescope and forget to see the object at which it is pointed. You can get caught up in praise and forget Him who is the focus of praise. Too often what occurs in worship services is the praise of praise or the joy of praise, but somehow it misses focusing on God, His supremacy, His passion for His name, and for His glory. Focus on Him even more than on His passion for His people and even more than all the peoples of the world around the throne worshiping Him. True worship involves submitting yourself to God, abdicating your own self, giving devotion to God, adoring Him, exalting Him, and glorifying Him.

God desires that His people glorify Him in all things. On earth you glorify God by worshiping Him. You glorify God as you let the glory of God shine to all corners of the globe. You glorify God by giving Him the credit for all that He has done. You honor Christ as a sovereign Lord as you confess Him, praise Him, and proclaim Him to all peoples of the world! The mission of God is that the knowledge of His glory will cover the earth as the water covers the sea. Your mission is to live God's purpose for His glory.

NOTES

CHAPTER 1, A ROAD MAP FOR THE JOURNEY

1. Ivey Harrington Beckman, compiler, "Family Album," *Home Life*, February 2001, 15.

CHAPTER 2, ABRAHAM ON MISSION WITH GOD—A BLESSING FOR ALL PEOPLES

1. Henry Blackaby, *Created to Be God's Friend: How God Shapes Those He Loves* (Nashville: Thomas Nelson, 1999).

2. *The Experiencing God Study Bible* (Nashville: Broadman & Holman Publishers, 1994), 179.

3. Thomas D. Elliff, *Praying for Others* (Nashville: Broadman Press, 1979), 79.

CHAPTER 7: PAUL ON MISSION WITH GOD—THE GOSPEL FOR ALL PEOPLES

1. See my book *Indonesian Revival: Why Two Million Came to Christ* (Pasadena, CA: William Carey Library, 1978).

CHAPTER 8, JOHN ON MISSION WITH GOD—
ALL PEOPLES WORSHIP GOD

1. Jeff Lewis, *God's Heart for the Nations* (Riverside, CA: The Global Center, California Baptist University, 2000), 24.

2. Arthur Percy Fitt, *Moody Still Lives: Words Pictures of D. L. Moody* (New York: Fleming H. Revell Co., 1936), 27–29.

3. John Piper, *Perspectives on the World Christian Movement* (Pasadena, CA:William Carey Library, 1991), 36.

4. Ibid., 39.